ARCHITETTI TIBILETTI ASSOCIATI

De aedibus

Der italienische Architekt und Architekturtheoretiker Aldo Rossi verglich die Architektur mit den Wissenschaften. Wie diese schreite die Architektur voran, indem sie stetig auf bereits Erreichtes aufbaue und sich so weiterentwickele. Diesem wissenschaftlichen Aspekt dient diese Buchreihe. Seit 2000 dokumentiert sie die aktuelle Schweizer Architektur. Die Reihe wird in ihrer Kontinuität gleichsam zu einem Gedächtnis der Architektur, das die Werke dem Vergessen entzieht. Von jedem der mit hohem Qualitätsanspruch ausgewählten Architekten und Architektenteams werden die wichtigsten Bauten festgehalten, ausführlich dargestellt und dokumentiert. Jeder Band dient auch der Reflexion über den architektonischen Willen, der hinter den Projekten steht. So sind in dieser Reihe mehr oder minder alle in der Schweiz wirkenden Architekturkritiker mit einzelnen oder mehreren Textbeiträgen vertreten.

Der Hauptteil in jedem Band widmet sich dagegen der Welt der Anschauung. So sind jeweils anhand von Bildern und Plänen einige bemerkenswerte Bauten dargestellt, die nicht einer routinierten «Produktion» entsprungen sind. Vielmehr steht hinter jedem Entwurf eine leidenschaftliche Auseinandersetzung mit der Aufgabe und deren Prämissen.

Heinz Wirz

De aedibus

The Italian architect and architectural theoretician Aldo Rossi compared architecture to the sciences. Like them, architecture progresses by constantly building upon what has already been achieved and develops further in this way. Since 2000, this series of books has been dedicated to the same academic approach in documenting contemporary Swiss architecture. It therefore becomes a form of architectural memory, ensuring that the architecture is not forgotten. The most important buildings by each of the selected high-quality architects are presented, described in detail and documented. Each volume also serves to reflect upon the architectural motivation behind the projects. By now, more or less every architectural critic working in Switzerland has contributed one or more articles to the series.

However, the core of each book is dedicated to the world of observation. Images and plans present a number of remarkable buildings that are not the result of routine "production". Instead, each design stems from a passionate engagement with the task and its premises.

Heinz Wirz

88 De aedibus

ARCHITETTI TIBILETTI ASSOCIATI

QUART

Alberto Caruso
DIE KLARHEIT DER ARCHITEKTONISCHEN FIGUR   6

Claudio Ferrata
INNERHALB DER LANDSCHAFTLICHEN MASSSTÄBE   16

AUFSTOCKUNG EINES WOHNGEBÄUDES UM EINE ZWEIGESCHOSSIGE   22
ATTIKA, VIA BUFFI, LUGANO

LABORE UND BÜROS AFLS, OLIVONE   26
in Zusammenarbeit mit Enrico Sassi Architetto, Lugano

UMBAU UND ERWEITERUNG DES WOHNGEBÄUDES CASA DOPPIA,   30
VIA DUFOUR, LUGANO

EINFAMILIENHAUS VILLA 101, VIA ALDESAGO, LUGANO   34

APARTMENTGEBÄUDE, VIA BELTRAMINA, LUGANO   40

AUFSTOCKUNG UND UMBAU EINES WOHN- UND GESCHÄFTSGEBÄUDES,   44
VICOLO NASSETTA, LUGANO

APARTMENTGEBÄUDE WESTSIDE 9, VIA SASSA, LUGANO   48

ERWEITERUNG UND UMBAU DES EHEMALIGEN RATHAUSES VON PREGASSONA   52
ZU EINER GRUNDSCHULE UND GEMEINDEÄMTERN, LUGANO

SENIORENRESIDENZ PARCO MOROSINI, AUFTRAG ZU EINER PARALLELSTUDIE: 56
AUSWAHLENTWURF, VEZIA

PARKHAUS OSPEDALE ITALIANO, VIA DEGLI ORTI, LUGANO   58
in Zusammenarbeit mit Remo Leuzinger Architetto, Lugano

ERWEITERUNG DES CASALE LA REPARATA, LUGANO-PREGASSONA   64

MEHRGENERATIONENQUARTIER PARCO SAN ROCCO, COLDRERIO   68

BIOGRAFIEN, WERKVERZEICHNIS, BIBLIOGRAFIE   72

Alberto Caruso
THE CLARITY OF THE ARCHITECTURAL FORM — 7

Claudio Ferrata
IN THE MIDST OF SCALES OF THE LANDSCAPE — 17

HEIGHTENING OF AN APARTMENT BUILDING WITH THE ADDITION OF A PENTHOUSE-DUPLEX, VIA BUFFI, LUGANO — 22

AFLS LABORATORIES AND OFFICES, OLIVONE — 26
Co-designer: Enrico Sassi Architetto, Lugano

RESTRUCTURING AND EXPANSION OF THE "CASA DOPPIA" APARTMENT BUILDING, VIA DUFOUR, LUGANO — 30

SINGLE-FAMILY HOME "VILLA 101", VIA ALDESAGO, LUGANO — 34

APARTMENT BUILDING, VIA BELTRAMINA, LUGANO — 40

HEIGHTENING AND RESTRUCTURING OF A COMMERCIAL AND RESIDENTIAL BUILDING, VICOLO NASSETTA, LUGANO — 44

"WESTSIDE 9" APARTMENT BUILDING, VIA SASSA, LUGANO — 48

EXTENSION AND CONVERSION OF THE FORMER PREGASSONA CITY HALL INTO AN ELEMENTARY SCHOOL AND MUNICIPAL OFFICES, LUGANO — 52

"PARCO MOROSINI" RESIDENCE FOR SELF-SUFFICIENT SENIORS PARALLEL STUDY MANDATES: SELECTED PROJECT VEZIA — 56

OSPEDALE ITALIANO CAR PARK, VIA DEGLI ORTI, LUGANO — 58
Co-designer: Remo Leuzinger Architetto, Lugano

"CASALE LA REPARATA" EXTENSION, PREGASSONA-LUGANO — 64

"PARCO SAN ROCCO" INTERGENERATIONAL DISTRICT, COLDRERIO — 68

BIOGRAPHIES, LIST OF WORKS, BIBLIOGRAPHY — 73

DIE KLARHEIT DER ARCHITEKTONISCHEN FIGUR

Alberto Caruso

Der Entwurf des Architekten für das eigene Wohnhaus verrät immer einen authentischen Aspekt seines Denkens. Mitunter handelt es sich um einen intimen, tiefgründigen Aspekt, den man einem Bauherrn gegenüber kaum zum Ausdruck bringen kann, oder man realisiert – in komprimierter, symbolischer Form – ein architektonisches Bestreben, das in vollem Umfang auszudrücken bis dahin die beruflichen Aufträge nicht zugelassen haben.

Das Haus von Stefano Tibiletti und Catherine Gläser Tibiletti in Lugano befindet sich direkt ausserhalb des kompakten Stadtkerns aus dem 20. Jahrhundert, wo sich Einzelhäuser aus den 1930er- bis 1950er-Jahren mit privaten Gärten abwechseln. Das vierstöckige Wohnhaus wurde um ein weiteres Geschoss aufgestockt, das die gleiche Gestalt der darunterliegenden Geschosse aufgreift. Auf der Dachterrasse entstand ein transparenter Baukörper zur Nutzung als grosser Wohnraum, von dem aus sich ein spektakulärer Blick über die Stadt – von den Bergen bis hin zum See – bietet und der nachts zu einer Art leuchtenden Laterne wird, was den Charakter des ursprünglichen Gebäudes verändert (Abb. 1).

Abb. 1 Aufstockung eines Wohngebäudes durch eine zweigeschossige Wohnung, Via Buffi, Lugano
Fig. 1 Apartment building heightened into a penthouse duplex, Via Buffi Lugano

Neben der kulturellen Ausbildung von Stefano Tibiletti und Catherine Gläser Tibiletti (beide haben die Architekturschule der Universität in Genf besucht, die damals Bruno Reichlin leitete), die auf dem Studium der Meister der Moderne gründete, entdeckt man bei ihnen vor allem eine starke Neigung zur Urbanität, die ihr Handwerk durchdringt. Es ist jene Urbanität, die die Tessiner Architekturkultur der Nachkriegszeit charakterisiert und die Werke der Architekten verbindet, die das Tessin über die Grenzen des Kontinents hinaus bekanntgemacht haben. Es waren Architekten mit unterschiedlichen Idealen und Formensprachen, jedoch vereint durch ihr gemeinsames Konzept, nämlich die Überzeugung, dass die Stadt die am stärksten entwickelte Art des Wohnens darstellt und der Gesellschaftsort schlechthin ist. Die Stadt als sich ständig verändernde Konstruktion, als ideales Terrain für ihren Beruf. Die Stadt als Lösung für die Befreiung der Gebiete, die von ungeordneter Expansion und Siedlungsausbreitung gefährdet sind. Die Stadt als Bestreben, in der Mehrheit der Fälle entmutigt durch das Fehlen beruflicher Gelegenheiten und durch die kulturpolitische Lage, die das Gelingen verschiedener gegensätzlicher Wohnmodelle begünstigt hat.

Die intensive und komplexe Beziehung zwischen den Werken der Tessiner Architekten aus den 1970er-Jahren und dem natürlichen Umfeld und der Topografie des Orts rührt von der Entwicklung des Stadtbegriffs her – und dem Druck, eine der Stadt angemessene Dichte herzustellen, die auf den landschaftlichen Kontext und die spärlich besiedelten Gebiete im Umfeld angepasst ist.

Im Öffentlichen Schwimmbad von Bellinzona (Aurelio Galfetti, Flora Ruchat-Roncati, Ivo Trümpy; 1970), dem vielsagendsten Werk aus jenen Jahren, führt der Fussgängersteg über die Badeanlage und verbindet die Stadt mit dem Fluss: Dies ist ein nie dagewesenes Zeichen von Urbanität und beinhaltet eine leibhaftige Idee von der Stadt. Der Massstabssprung sorgt dafür, dass das Öffentliche Schwimmbad vollständig zur Stadt, zu ihrem dichten, historisch gewachsenen System von Beziehungen gehört.

In den 1960er- und 1970er-Jahren boten die kleinen Tessiner Städte keine Wohnhäuser, die dem neuen Anspruch des jungen Tessiner Bürgertums, das sich infolge der wirtschaftlichen Nachkriegsentwicklung herausgebildet hatte, entsprachen. Das Modell

THE CLARITY OF THE ARCHITECTURAL FORM

Alberto Caruso

An architect's design for his own home always reveals some authentic aspect of his thinking. At times it is something intimate and profound, not easily expressed in designs for clients, or it is a contracted and symbolic form of an architectural aspiration that, until that moment, could not be fully expressed through the professional opportunities.

The Lugano home of Stefano Tibiletti and Catherine Gläser Tibiletti is just outside the compact 20th-century city, where isolated buildings constructed between the 1930s and 1950s alternate with private gardens. The four-storeyed residential building was raised by one level, with the same configuration as the lower floors. A transparent volume intended for use as a large living space was then built on the rooftop terrace. It has a spectacular view of the city – from the mountains to the lake – and at night, becomes a luminous lantern, transfiguring the character of the pre-existing building (*Fig. 1*).

In addition to Stefano and Catherine's cultural education (both studied at the University of Geneva, directed at that time by Bruno Reichlin), with study of the modernist masters providing the foundation, what comes through first and foremost is the strong propensity toward urbanity that runs through their profession. That urbanity characterized the Ticinese architectural culture following the war and is a common element in the works of those who brought Ticino to the awareness of the world beyond continental boundaries. Architects with different poetics and languages, united by a shared concept: the conviction that the city was the most evolved place for habitation and the social space par excellence. The city as a construction in constant transformation, an ideal terrain for the profession. The city re-proposed as a solution for redeeming territories that had been compromised by random expansion and urban sprawl. The city as an aspiration, in most cases disheartened by the lack of professional opportunities and the political and cultural condition that fostered the success of diverse and opposing housing models.

The intense and complex relationship between works by Ticinese architects of the 1970s and the surrounding nature and topographical footprints of the sites are derived from a developing notion of the city – and the propensity for creating a density of relationships between the city – and the natural landscapes and underpopulated areas.

In the Bellinzona Public Swimming Pool (Aurelio Galfetti, Flora Ruchat-Roncati, Ivo Trümpy; 1970), the most eloquent work of those years, the walkway that passes above the complex to connect the city to the river is an unprecedented gesture of urbanity, underpinning a real and true idea of a city. It is the leap and scale that makes the Public Swimming Pool fully belong to the city, to its dense and historically stratified system of relationships.

In the 1960s and 1970s, the small cities in Ticino had no housing supply to meet the new demands of Ticino's younger middle class, educated during the economic boom of the post-war period. The suburban single-family dwelling model adopted by the new classes, masterfully interpreted by the new architects, was shared by all classes in the years to follow and, nurtured by credit and the liberal urban planning policy, slowly invaded the valleys and lakeshores.

des ausserhalb der Stadt gelegenen Einfamilienhauses für neue Bevölkerungsschichten, von neuen Architekten virtuos interpretiert, wurde in den folgenden Jahren von allen Schichten bewohnt und hat, gefördert durch Glaubwürdigkeit und eine liberale Städtebaupolitik, langsam das Gebiet der Talsohlen und Seeufer überschwemmt. Zwischen den städtischen Bestrebungen der Architekturkultur und der Realität der territorialen Bedingung hat sich daher eine wachsende problematische Distanz herausgebildet: eine Distanz, die man heute bei den Angeboten der kultivierten Architekten und den Immobilienstrategien registriert, die darauf ausgerichtet sind, der weitverbreiteten Nachfrage nachzukommen. Die Arbeit von Architetti Tibiletti Associati ist von diesen Bestrebungen gekennzeichnet. Sie haben sich für ein Leben in der Stadt entschieden und ihr Haus über einem anderen errichtet, und dies mit einer eindeutigen Geste zugunsten der Stadt, der Dichte und des urbanen gesellschaftlichen Zusammenlebens.

Von den in Lugano ausgeführten Bauwerken ist die – 2009 in demselben Viertel wie ihr eigenes Wohnhaus errichtete – Casa Doppia (Abb. 2) vielleicht diejenige Architektur, die am besten ihr Planungsverhalten veranschaulicht. Das kleine Gebäude aus dem 20. Jahrhundert mit strengem, bürgerlichem Erscheinungsbild wurde umgebaut und durch eine moderne Erweiterung in Form eines zweiten Baukörpers verdoppelt. Der neue Baukörper ist eine autonome Architektur, nur eine einzige vertikale Verbindung erschliesst die beiden Wohneinheiten. Der einfache und äusserst zweckmässige Grundriss der Erweiterung verteilt sich auf einen fabrikartigen Baukörper mit einer kleinen Grundfläche im Querschnitt. Dieser ist genauso weit von der Strassenflucht zurückgesetzt, dass er optisch unabhängig wirkt, was die zusätzlichen zwei Geschosse noch betonen. Die Front zur Strasse hin präsentiert sich fensterlos, während sich die Wohnräume durch eine Reihe übereinander angeordneter Loggien zum Stadtzentrum hin öffnen. Die grosse Seitenfront ist durch stringente horizontale Fensterbänder gegliedert, die ganz klar die Formensprache der traditionellen rationalistischen Architektur in Mitteleuropa in Erinnerung rufen. Die Dachterrasse bietet eine schöne Aussicht auf die Stadt. Ihre besondere Wirkung wird durch die Öffnung der Wand zur Strassenseite hin mit einem zusätzlichen Ausblick zum See betont. Neben dem Verweis auf die weisse Architektur der 1930er-Jahre offenbart die Casa Doppia anhand der Behandlung der Oberflächen und anhand der ursprünglichen Klarheit des Grundrisses zudem den Einfluss der neuen iberischen Architektur – die in der Zeit der Erbauung einen grossen medienwirksamen Erfolg erlebte. Dies erklärt sich nicht zuletzt durch die Nähe Stefano Tibilettis zu Manuel und Francisco Aires Mateus, deren Assistent er an der Accademia di Architettura in Mendrisio war. Der entscheidendste Punkt, der sich an der Casa Doppia zeigt, ist die Haltung gegenüber dem Bestehenden, ist die Sorgfalt, mit der Architetti Tibiletti Associati das alte Gebäude umgebaut haben. Dabei haben sie seinen architektonischen Charakter durch den Neubau trotz dessen expliziter Modernität nicht angetastet, sondern aufgewertet.

Abb. 2 Sanierung und Erweiterung des Wohngebäudes Casa Doppia, Via Doufur, Lugano
Fig. 2 Renovation and extension of the "Casa Doppia" apartment block, Via Doufur, Lugano

Die Residenza Galleria ist ein weiterer Bau in der Stadt (Abb. 3), der an der Seepromenade von Lugano liegt. Auch in diesem Fall handelt es sich um ein historisches Gebäude – mit einer geordnet und ruhig dekorierten Front –, das renoviert und erweitert wurde. Die Aufstockung bildet eine neue auffällige Bekrönung, die über dem Mauervorsprung mit Dachtraufe errichtet wurde und auf der Vorgängerarchitektur auflagert, ohne die kompositorischen Zusammenhänge zu stören. Livio Vacchini – bei dem Stefano Tibiletti seine ersten beruflichen Schritte ging – behauptete, dass sich bei Stadtgebäuden die Funktion des Sockels nach der klassischen Dreiteilung der Fronten (Sockel, Rumpf und Bekrönung) aus dem künstlichen Boden heraus entwickelt – ein weitverbreitetes Element in der Stadtsituation – und dass folglich bei der Planung auf

Abb. 3 Aufstockung und Umbau eines Wohn- und Geschäftshauses, Vicolo Nassetta, Lugano
Fig. 3 Heightening and renovation of a commercial and residential building, Vicolo Nassetta, Lugano

A widening and problematic gap has formed between the urban design aspirations of the architectural culture and the reality of the territorial condition. A gap that exists today between the proposals of erudite architects and real estate strategies aimed at satisfying the most widespread demand. The work of Tibiletti Associati is distinguished by these aspirations. They chose to live in the city and build their house on top of another house, in an unequivocal gesture that favours the city, density and urban sociability.

Of the projects executed in Lugano, Casa Doppia (*Fig. 2*) – built in 2009 in the same neighbourhood as their home – is perhaps the architecture that most eloquently represents their attitude toward design. The small, austere, respectable 20th-century building was renovated and doubled with a modern extension consisting of a second volume. The new building is an autonomous architectural form, while a single vertical connection serves both housing units. In the layout of the basic and extremely rationalist extension, the narrower building is set just far enough back from the line of the road to give it figurative independence, which is emphasized by that fact that it has two storeys more than the pre-existing building.

The side bordering the road is windowless, while the living rooms open onto a series of loggias, one on top of another, orientated towards the city centre. The large wall on the internal side is slashed horizontally by a tight row of ribbon windows, explicitly recalling the Central European rationalist language. The rooftop terrace is a panoramic lookout over the city, its function exalted by the irregular form of the wall facing the street, which has a view towards the lake. Aside from the reference to the white architecture of the 1930s, Casa Doppia, in the treatment of the surfaces and in the original clarity of the plan, reveals a suggestion of new Iberian architecture – which in that period was highly successful in the media. Stefano is familiar with the work of Manuel and Francisco Aires Mateus, for whom he worked as an assistant at the Academy of Architecture in Mendrisio. The most relevant issue with Casa Doppia is the attitude towards the original building and the care taken by the Tibiletti architects in transforming the old building. Its architectural character was not tampered with, but enhanced by the new building, which in turn has not renounced the affirmation of its modernity.

Residenza Galleria is another work, a city building (*Fig. 3*) situated on the shores of Lake Lugano. Here is another heritage building – its façade decorated in an orderly and quiet fashion – which was renovated and extended. By heightening the building, a striking new capital was created, built out beyond the overhang of the eaves and overlapping with the existing architecture without damaging its compositional relationships. Livio Vacchini – with whom Stefano first practised his profession – maintained that with city buildings, the role of the base in the classic tripartite division of the façades (base, shaft and capital) is played by the man-made ground, a common element in urban areas. Thus its design must aim at a careful relationship between the shaft and the capital, as well as the building's relationship to the sky. The series of large windows that, like a meander or Greek key pattern, complete the Residenza Galleria, giving it an elegance capable of competing with the other different buildings in the row, with their elaborate forms, by means of a simple architectural artifice.

Again in the city of Lugano, the building on Via Beltramina is another example of a distributive rationale, with a cladding whose morphology differs

das Verhältnis zwischen Rumpf und Aufbau und auf die Beziehung zwischen Bauwerk und Himmel geachtet werden müsse. Die Abfolge von grossen Fenstern, die wie ein Mäanderband den oberen Abschluss der Residenza Galleria bilden, verleihen dem Bau ein elegantes Erscheinungsbild, das – in einer relativ schlichten Architektur – mit den anderen Gebäuden der Strassenfront, die überbordende Formen aufweisen, konkurrieren kann.

Von den Stadtbauten in Lugano ist das Haus in der Via Beltramina ein weiteres Beispiel für eine Zweckmässigkeit in der Raumaufteilung innerhalb einer Gebäudehülle, die eine ganz andere Morphologie aufweist als die bis dahin errichteten Bauten. Das an der Strasse gelegene Haus steht der eindrucksvollen kompositen Front des grossen, 1995 von Mario Campi und Franco Pessina errichteten Wohngebäudes gegenüber und bildet als Reaktion darauf einen perfekt quaderförmigen Monolithen aus, der nur im Bereich des Eingangs ausgehöhlt ist. Zahlreiche kleine Öffnungen in drei Formaten, die frei über den Baukörper verteilt sind, durchbrechen die perfekte Geometrie, sodass sie seinen kompakten Gesamteindruck nicht stören. Die Form des durchlöcherten monolithischen Baus findet man häufig in der internationalen Architektur. Er stellt ein introvertiertes Bauwerk dar, das keine wesentlichen Bezüge sucht und unumstösslich seine Distanz zu dem Bauwerk von Campi und Pessina behauptet.

Abb. 4 Einfamilienhaus, Cureglia
Fig. 4 Single family dwelling, Cureglia

Dieses Gebäude zeigt ganz deutlich die Neigung von Architetti Tibiletti Associati zu einem unbefangenen und kontrollierten Empirismus, zu der Fähigkeit, eklektische Streifzüge in selbst von der Tessiner Moderne entfernte architektonische Räume zu organisieren und dabei diese Beispiele immer auf eine rigorose, kohärente Geometrie, auf eine Rationalität zurückzuführen, die den unverrückbaren Hintergrund ihres Berufs darstellt.

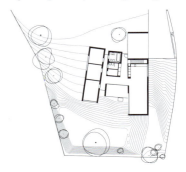

Abb. 5 Erdgeschoss des Einfamilienhauses, Cureglia
Fig. 5 Ground floor, single family dwelling, Cureglia

Die Casa Cureglia von 2004 (*Abb.* 4 und 5) ist das erste Werk, bei dem die Architekten diese Haltung klar und massgeblich zum Ausdruck bringen. Die drei «Trakte» – wie Livio Vacchini sie bezeichnete – sind auf dem Gelände in flachen Winkeln zueinander positioniert. Motiviert durch die Raumverteilung und die Beziehung zur Landschaft, lassen die verschiedenen Gebäudeteile Verbindungsräume von unerwarteter Wirkung entstehen, die dem kleinen Haus eine ungewöhnliche Räumlichkeit verleihen. Die iberische Architektur – deren Anziehungskraft durch die Eigentümlichkeit eines «kritischen Regionalismus» parallel zum Tessiner Regionalismus begründet ist – stellt eine wichtige Inspirationsquelle in ihrer Arbeit dar. Der Portikus der Casa Duplo, die 2004 in Zusammenarbeit mit Enrico Sassi entstanden ist (*Abb.* 6), erinnert an die Form des Portikus der Universität von Aveiro von Álvaro Siza Vieira (*Abb.* 7). Der portugiesische Architekt hat gelehrt, wie einige kontrollierte Ausgliederungen sowie leichte Abweichungen von der Linienführung – wie bei der Casa Cureglia – bedeutende räumliche Effekte sowohl im Innenraum als auch im Verhältnis zum Umfeld erzielen können.

Abb. 6 Einfamilienhaus Casa Duplo, Cureglia
Fig. 6 Casa Duplo single family dwelling, Cureglia

Die kultiviert-eklektische Praxis von Architetti Tibiletti Associati hat dazu geführt, dass sie untereinander verschiedene und gegensätzliche volumetrische Figuren ausprobieren, wie etwa bei den Abweichungen in der Linienführung bei der Casa Cureglia im Vergleich zu dem monolithischen Baukörper des Hauses in der Via Beltramina in Lugano. Bei der Villa 101 in Aldesago wurde der monolithische Baukörper in eine Abfolge durch Lichtschächte getrennter Einheiten aufgegliedert, sodass sich die Villa in der Landschaft kompositorisch aus fünf kleinen, zwischen Vollform und Leerform alternierenden Volumina zusammengesetzt präsentiert. An die Stelle von weissem Putz ist Sichtbeton mit einer feinen, perfekten Oberfläche getreten, wie er in der Tessiner Tradition besonders beliebt ist. Der Sichtbeton verleiht einer Architektur, deren Qualität auf der reinen Geometrie des Entwurfs gründet, mehr als jedes andere

Abb. 7 Álvaro Siza Vieira, Universität Aveiro, Aveiro
Fig. 7 Alvaro Siza University, Aveiro

from those used until now. Located directly on the road, it interacts with the imposing and composite façade of the large residential building designed by Campi and Pessina in 1995. It reacts as a perfect parallelepiped monolith, carved out only in the corner at the entrance. The perfect geometry is punctured by numerous small openings in three formats, freely distributed so as not to unbalance the whole. The perforated monolith is often used on the international architectural scene. It is an introverted work, which does not seek important relationships, peremptorily affirming its distance from the Campi and Pessina building.

This building clearly reveals the Tibiletti architects' inclination towards an uninhibited and controlled empiricism, towards being able to organize eclectic incursions into architectural spaces even far from Ticino's modernity, always bringing these experiments back to a strict and coherent geometry, to a rationalist approach that is the constant background to their work.

Casa Cureglia of 2004 (*Fig. 4, 5*) is the first work in which the architects express this attitude clearly and with authority. The three "tubes" – as Livio Vacchini called them – are positioned on the ground at slight angles. Motivated by reasons of distribution and the relationship with the landscape, the different angles create spaces whose relationship has an unexpected effect, giving the small house an unusual spatiality. Iberian architecture – whose attraction lies in the unique and "critical regionalism" parallel to that of Ticino - is an important source of inspiration in their work. The portico of Casa Duplo, of 2004 (designed in collaboration with E. Sassi) (*Fig. 6*), recalls the shape of the portico of the University of Aveiro by Alvaro Siza (*Fig. 7*). The Portuguese master taught that some controlled misalignments and slight deformations in the layout angles can have important spatial effects – as with Casa Cureglia – both in the interior space and in relationship to the surroundings.

The eruditely eclectic practice of the Tibiletti architects led them to experiment with different and opposing volumetric forms, as in Casa Cureglia's misalignments with respect to the monolithic house on Via Beltramina. In the Villa 101 in Aldesago, the monolith was fragmented into a series of units separated by shafts of light, offering the landscape the compositional narrative of the five small volumes alternating between filled areas and voids, into which the house is divided. The white plaster has become exposed concrete, with as perfect and refined a surface as the most celebrated traditional Ticinese material. More than any other material, exposed concrete provides the precision and solidity required for an architecture that bases its quality on the clear geometry of the design. A clarity that would not be achievable without details dictated by an extensive technical knowledge.

The car park of the Italian Hospital is also a monolith, made with a cladding of metal strips, but in this case, the point where the structure meets the ground becomes a way to relate with the city. The basement, penetrated by a public path, houses spaces for meetings and conferences, as well as access to the car park. Not only does the infrastructure for mobility perform the task it was primarily intended for – parking spaces – but it is also an active element of urban life. The functional mix promotes a multi-storey car park in urban architecture.

The mastery with which the architects manipulate various references and experiment with different morphologies is made possible by the fact that they

Material die nötige Präzision und Solidität – eine Reinheit, die ohne Details, bedingt durch ein starkes technisches Wissen, nicht realisierbar wäre.

Auch das Parkhaus des Ospedale Italiano in Lugano ist ein Monolith mit einer Hülle aus Metallprofilen, doch in diesem Fall ist die Verankerung im Gelände zu einem Instrument der Anbindung an die Stadt geworden. Der Sockel, durch den eine Fussgängerunterführung verläuft, beherbergt Versammlungs- und Konferenzräume sowie die Zugänge zum Parkhaus. Die Mobilitätsinfrastruktur erfüllt nicht nur ihre Hauptaufgabe – die Unterbringung von Autos –, sondern ist zugleich ein aktives Element der Urbanität. Die Funktionsmischung macht aus dem Parkhaus eine städtische Architektur.

Die Meisterschaft, mit der die Architekten verschiedene Bezüge manipulieren und mit unterschiedlichen Morphologien experimentieren, ermöglicht ihre starke Verankerung in den Grundlagen der Tessiner Moderne. Die Stirnseite des kleinen Anbaus an La Reparata in Pregassona ist eine wahrhafte Hommage an die kühle Formensprache der ersten Werke Luigi Snozzis.

Stefano Tibiletti ist ein Sohn der Kunst, sein Vater Alberto Tibiletti ist ein Architekt aus der gleichen Generation wie Luigi Snozzi und Livio Vacchini, mit dem zusammen er von 1973 bis 1975 das Macconi-Kaufhaus im Zentrum von Lugano entworfen hat (Abb. 8). 25 Jahre später – im Jahr 2000 – wurde das Gebäude von Vacchini zusammen mit Alberto und dem jungen Büro Architetti Tibiletti Associati um einen Anbau erweitert, der die Entwicklung der Tessiner Architektur überzeugend repräsentiert. Alberto Tibiletti hat viele bedeutende Bauten errichtet, die genaue Zeugnisse der rationalistischen Kultur sind.

Der kultivierte Eklektizismus von Architetti Tibiletti Associati ist eine Haltung, die sich in der Tessiner Moderne seit den Architekten der ersten Generation findet. Rino Tami, Franco Ponti, Peppo Brivio, Augusto Jäggli, Alberto Camenzind haben die Moderne entdeckt, indem sie sich an die verschiedenen Formensprachen der europäischen Architekten aus den ersten Jahrzehnten des 20. Jahrhunderts angelehnt haben. Die grossen Architekten der 1960er- und 1970er-Jahre – die Architekten, die durch die Zürcher Ausstellung *Tendenzen – Neuere Architektur im Tessin* 1975 zu internationalen Ehren kamen – orientierten sich an Le Corbusier, Ludwig Mies van der Rohe, Alvar Aalto, Louis I. Kahn und übertrugen deren Schöpfungen auf den Massstab der Tessiner Landschaft. Die starken, auch ethischen Elemente, die sie sich aneigneten, verbergen niemals die Unterschiede zwischen ihren Formensprachen, sodass man nicht von einer «Tessiner Schule» sprechen kann, wie nunmehr alle Kritiker einhellig der Meinung sind.

Abb. 8 Kaufhaus Macconi, Lugano
Fig. 8 **Macconi Centre, Lugano**

Die Architekturkultur im Tessin in diesen letzten Jahren durchlebt eine Phase des Suchens und ist zu einem Labor geworden, das für Experimente in verschiedene Richtungen offen ist. Die Protagonisten dieser Phase sind die «kultivierten Architekten», die an Wettbewerben teilnehmen und diese mit der Realisierung öffentlicher Bauten auch gewinnen und die zumeist von dem Markt der Architekten ausgeschlossen sind, derer sich Immobiliengruppen spekulativer Immobiliengeschäfte bedienen. Die Suche nach neuen Wegen wird bei der Arbeit dieser Architekten von dem «Widerstand» der von den Meistern geerbten Prinzipien begleitet.

Die Einfachheit als Endergebnis eines mühsamen Wegs, der Rückgriff auf die Geometrie und auf die Kohärenz ihrer Regeln, die Ablehnung der Architektur als spektakuläre Zurschaustellung, die Strenge bei der Raumaufteilung und die zielgerichtete technische Suche nach dem Raumergebnis sind die zentralen Themen dieser Architekten.

Einige wollen den Gedanken Luigi Snozzis aktualisieren, andere widmen sich einer weitreichenderen und zwangloseren Formensuche. Das, was sie jedoch eint, ist

are well anchored in the foundations of Ticinese modernity. The façade of the small extension of La Reparata, in Pregassona, is a true homage to the dry language of Luigi Snozzi's early works.

Stefano was born into the profession. His father Alberto is an architect of the same generation as Snozzi and Vacchini, with whom he designed the Macconi building (*Fig. 8*) in the centre of Lugano in 1973–1975. Twenty-five years later, in 2000, the building was expanded by Vacchini, along with Alberto and the young Tibiletti, an extension that eloquently represents the evolution of Ticino's architecture. Alberto Tibiletti built many important buildings, precise evidence of the rationalist culture.

The erudite eclecticism of the Tibiletti architects is a widespread attitude in the modernist architecture of Ticino, starting with the first generation architects. Rino Tami, Franco Ponti, Peppo Brivio, Augusto Jäggli and Alberto Camenzind discovered modernist architecture by exploring the different languages of the European masters in the early decades of the 20th century. The masters of the 1960s and 1970s, those of the "Tendenzia", looked to Le Corbusier, Mies, Aalto and Kahn, translating their poetics to the scale of the Ticinese landscape. The strong, even ethical common elements never hide the differences in their languages, so one cannot talk about the "Ticinese school", as all critics now agree.

In recent years, the Ticinese architectural culture has been experiencing a research phase, becoming a laboratory open to experiments of various kinds. The protagonists of this phase are the "erudite architects", those who participate in competitions and win them by creating public works, and who, for the most part, are excluded from the professional market used by speculative real estate groups. In the work of these architects, the quest for new pathways is accompanied by the "resistance" of the principles inherited from the masters.

Simplicity as the final outcome of a strenuous journey, the use of geometry and the consistency of its rules, architecture's refusal to be a spectacular exhibition, distributional rigor and technical research aimed at the spatial outcome.

Some strive to bring Luigi Snozzi's thinking up to date. Others are dedicated to a broader and more casual linguistic research. What they have in common, however, is the rationalist motivation on which any form must be founded. Architecture must be intelligible. It must be possible to recognize the principles directly in its forms, which must be comprehensible, in this way fulfilling the civic aspect of the profession. One quality of the Tibiletti architects' work is "comprehensibility". In their projects, the architectural form is elementary and communicative.

Among the latest works, the project for the intergenerational district of Coldrerio, in Mendrisiotto, shows a leap in scale and indicates that the profession is slowly changing, offering more complex design opportunities aimed at transforming vaster segments of the territory. In addition to the new care home for the elderly, the competition included social and community activity spaces, housing, and a reorganization of the open public spaces: an urban-scale project to create a system of spatial relationships that makes the village's central area denser, designing a small piece of city. The intelligent planivolumetric proposal includes plans for adopting the layout of the existing municipal building and school, as well as locating the main building in the green area behind

die rationale Motivation, auf der jede Form gründen muss. Architektur muss verständlich sein. Es muss möglich sein, die Grundlagen direkt an ihren Formen zu erkennen, die nachvollziehbar sein müssen, um so die soziale Dimension des Berufs zu verwirklichen. «Verständlichkeit» ist eine Qualität, die sich in der Arbeit von Architetti Tibiletti Associati zeigt, bei ihren Entwürfen ist die architektonische Figur elementar und kommunikativ.

Von den letzten Arbeiten zeigt der Entwurf für das Mehrgenerationenquartier in Coldrerio im Umfeld von Mendrisio einen Massstabssprung und signalisiert, dass die beruflichen Bedingungen langsam im Wandel begriffen sind, da sich komplexere Projektmöglichkeiten bieten, welche die Umwandlung grösserer Grundstücke zum Ziel haben. Neben dem neuen Seniorenheim sah der Wettbewerb auch Räumlichkeiten für Aktivitäten zur gesellschaftlichen Eingliederung, Wohnungen sowie eine städtebauliche Neuordnung der öffentlichen Aussenräume vor. Es war ein Projekt städtischen Massstabs zur Realisierung eines räumlichen Bezugssystems, das das zentrale Gebiet der Siedlung verdichtet und dabei einen kleinen Teil der Stadt entwirft. Der intelligente Lageplan sieht vor, das bestehende Gemeindehaus und die Schule an ihrer Position zu belassen und das Hauptgebäude auf die rückwärtige Grünfläche zu stellen, um so eine exakte Grenze, auch in der Höhe, zwischen dem öffentlichen Park und dem neuen Fussgängerbereich zu etablieren. Der so entstandene Platz wird zum Verbindungspunkt zwischen den Aktivitäten in den neuen und in bereits bestehenden Gebäuden.

Die Zweckmässigkeit der Raumverteilung, die bislang auf verschiedene Art und Weise im Inneren der Gebäude erprobt wurde, wird hier nun auf die Anordnung der Aussenräume angewandt. Der Akzent der Projektentwicklung liegt auf den Leerräumen, die den Entwurf dominieren und dessen Qualität ausmachen. Das Raumkonzept ist so wichtig, dass die architektonische Komposition der Fronten in den Hintergrund rückt: Das Raster aus horizontalen Gurtbändern und vertikalen Fenster- und Türreihen – wie sie bereits in der Residenza Parco Morosini zum Einsatz kamen – erfüllt die Aufgabe mit expressiver Ökonomie.

Die Herausforderung, die heute die Forschung beschäftigt – und die eine wahrhaftige Zeit der Erneuerung für den «kritischen Regionalismus» im Tessin eröffnen kann –, besteht in der grossmassstäblichen Planung. Die Umkehrung der Tendenz zur Siedlungsverbreitung, die Stärkung der Städte, um die Rückkehr der Bewohner der Stadtrandgebiete zu begünstigen, sind Perspektiven, die realistisch verfolgt werden können, wenn der Beitrag der Architekturkultur zum Protagonisten avanciert.

it, establishing a precise boundary, also in terms of altitude, between the public park and the new pedestrian area. The square that is then created establishes the relationship between the activities housed in the new buildings and those accommodated in the existing buildings.

The distributive rationale experimented thus far in different ways on the interior of the buildings is reversed in the layout of the open spaces. In the design's inventiveness, the accent is placed on the voids, which dominate the design and determine its quality. The spatial concept is so important that the architectural composition of the façades fades into the background: the grid of horizontal string courses and vertical rows of windows – already tried in the Residenza Parco Morosini – accomplishes the task with expressive economy.

The challenge facing research today – and which could be the start of a real season of change and innovation for Ticino's "critical regionalism" – is large-scale planning. Reversing the urban sprawl trend and reinforcing cities to encourage residents to return from peripheral areas are perspectives that can be realistically pursued, if the architectural culture is able to take the lead.

INNERHALB DER LANDSCHAFTLICHEN MASSSTÄBE

Claudio Ferrata

Wie soll man die Arbeit von Architetti Tibiletti Associati in Worte fassen? Aus einem einfachen Kompetenzgrund möchte ich versuchen, die Realisierungen des Büros in einen kulturellen Kontext einzuordnen, insbesondere will ich seine architektonische Arbeit mit den Begriffen «Landschaft», «Palimpsest» und «Territorium» in Verbindung bringen. Obwohl die Architekten Stefano Tibiletti und Catherine Gläser Tibiletti hauptsächlich im Tessin tätig sind und engen Kontakt zu der zuweilen fälschlich bezeichneten «Tessiner Schule» haben, konnten sie durch ihre gemeinsame Ausbildung in Genf einen Blick von aussen erwerben. Mounir Ayoub hat sich jüngst im Editorial der Ausgabe 23/24 der Schweizer Zeitschrift *Tracés* (2017) die Frage gestellt: Gibt es eine «Genfer Schule»? Seine Antwort fiel positiv aus. Was wären ihre Charakteristika? Die Genfer Schule zeichnet sich durch die Beachtung der städtebaulichen und landschaftlichen Dimension, durch eine kritische Haltung und ein Interesse an dem gesellschaftlichen Kontext aus, in dem sich das Handeln des Architekten abspielt. Die Lehren von Persönlichkeiten wie Bruno Reichlin, der lange Zeit die Hochschule leitete, Georges Descombes, Alain Léveillé, Riccardo Mariani, Giairo Daghini, Tita Carloni, Jacques Gubler und Bernardo Secchi, die Stefano Tibiletti und Catherine Gläser Tibiletti an der Ecole d'architecture de l'Université de Génève (EAUG) persönlich erleben und verfolgen konnten, haben das Paar sicher geprägt. Anschliessend machten sie dann andere Erfahrungen. Sie haben mit Secchi in Florenz und mit Livio Vacchini in Lugano zusammengearbeitet. Ausserdem hatte Stefano Tibiletti während seiner zeitweiligen Tätigkeit im Büro von Hans Kollhoff in Berlin die Gelegenheit, an grossen Wettbewerben im Zusammenhang mit der städtebaulichen Erneuerung der Stadt in den ersten Jahren nach dem Mauerfall mitzuwirken.

Tracés 23-24/2017, Genfer Schule
Tracés 23-24/2017, Geneva school

Der Standort eines Gebäudes ist immer reich an Natur- und Gesellschaftsgeschichte, an Zeichen und Werten, und er darf nicht auf einen einfachen physischen Ort reduziert werden, für den ein Projekt entsteht, oder auf einen einfachen Träger. Er ist nicht nur der Raum, auf den ein Planungskonzept angewendet wird, sondern er muss als eine Qualität, ein Potenzial betrachtet werden. Ich denke, es ist richtig zu behaupten, dass sich die Arbeit des Büros Architetti Tibiletti Associati in ihren verschiedenen Ausprägungen in eine derartige Logik einfügt. Nehmen wir nur den Entwurf für ein Wohnhaus am Hang des Monte Bré in Aldesago. Die Villa 101 befindet sich in einer Position, die wir als «heikel» bezeichnen könnten. Vor ihr breitet sich nämlich jene «grand paysage» aus, die den Luganersee, die umliegenden Berge und die Stadt Lugano einschliesst. Wie soll man diese Landschaft, die unmittelbar nahe als auch die weiter entfernte, und den Horizont beherrschen, ohne ein triviales Werk zu produzieren? Der Entwurf ist so angelegt, dass man diese Landschaft schrittweise entdeckt, und zwar durch die Wegführung, die am strasserseitigen Eingang ihren Anfang nimmt, durch eine Reihe von unterirdischen Räumen verläuft, bis man in das eigentliche Wohnhaus gelangt und von dort hinaus in den Garten. Auf diese Art und Weise offenbart sich die Landschaft. Wechseln wir nun in das städtische Umfeld von Molino Nuovo, einem volkstümlichen Viertel, wo das erste Wachstum der Stadt Lugano erfolgte und das heute sehr dynamisch geworden ist. Hier steht in der Via Beltramina 19 a+b ein Apartmentgebäude, das kleine Wohnungen und «Lofts» beherbergt. Es fügt sich in ein dichtes städtisches Gefüge mit einer klar abgegrenzten Parzellierung ein, die das neue Gebäude überzeugend komplettiert. Oder verlagern wir uns noch weiter nach

Luftaufnahme von Mendrisiotto, Kanton Tessin
Aerial photograph of Mendrisiotto, Canton of Ticino, Switzerland

IN THE MIDST OF SCALES OF THE LANDSCAPE

Claudio Ferrata

What to say about the work of Architetti Tibiletti Associati? Merely to answer this question professionally, I would like to try and provide a cultural context to the studio's achievements and in particular, I wish to discuss the architectural work in relation to notions of landscapes, palimpsests and territories. Although they have primarily worked in Ticino, maintaining solid contacts with what is sometimes called the "Ticino school", both architects trained in Geneva, allowing them to acquire an external vision. Recently, in the editorial of Issue 23–24 of the Swiss review *Tracés* (2017), Mounir Ayoub asked, "Y a-t-il une école de Genève?" ("Is there a Geneva school?") His answer was "yes". What are its characteristics? The "Geneva school" is characterized by a focus on urban and landscape dimensions, a critical attitude and an interest in the social context of the place in which the architect's practice is located. The teachings of the likes of Bruno Reichlin, who ran the school at the time, Georges Descombes, Alain Léveillé, Riccardo Mariani, Giairo Daghini, Tita Carloni, Jacques Gubler and Bernardo Secchi, under whom Stefano Tibiletti and Catherine Gläser Tibiletti were able to study at the Ecole d'architecture de l'Université de Genève (EAUG), certainly influenced the couple. They then gained more experience, working with Secchi in Florence and Livio Vacchini in Locarno. Stefano's time in Berlin at Hans Kollhoff's studio also allowed him to work on major competitions involving the city's urban renewal in the first years following the fall of the wall.

A building site is a point that is dense with natural and social history, loaded with signs and values, and should not be seen reductively as a mere physical place where a project is registered or as a simple support. Not only is it the space where a plan is carried out, but it must also be seen as potential. I think it is correct to say that the work of Architetti Tibiletti Associati, in its various forms, follows this kind of logic. Let us take the design of a house on the slopes of Monte Bré, in Aldesago. Villa 101 is located in a position that we could call "awkward". In fact, it looks upon that "grand paysage", that vast landscape which includes the gulf, the surrounding mountains and the city of Lugano. How is it possible to control this landscape, with its near and distant horizons, without producing a banal work? The design makes it possible to gradually discover the landscape along the path leading from the roadside access, passing through a series of underground spaces, up to the house entrance, before opening out into the garden, revealing a view of the landscape. Let us move on to an urban setting, to Molino Nuovo, a popular neighbourhood where the city of Lugano saw its first growth and which has become extremely dynamic. The Via Beltramina 19a+b building is located there and consists of small apartments and lofts. It is set in a dense fabric, with a clearly legible plot, which is convincingly occupied and completed by the new building. Or we could move on to Coldrerio, something of an urban sprawl where partial traces of the region's agricultural past can still be found in a haphazard context. The project under construction for the intergenerational neighbourhood, in an area with several municipal buildings, is characterized by public spaces and gardens that connect the new buildings, consisting of a multi-purpose community

Coldrerio in eine städtebaulich diffuse Situation, wo die Spuren der landwirtschaftlichen Vergangenheit der Region teilweise noch in einem ungeordneten Umfeld zu sehen sind. Das Projekt für das im Bau befindliche Mehrgenerationenquartier, das auf einem Gelände mit einigen bereits existierenden Gemeindebauten entsteht, zeichnet sich durch öffentliche Räume und Parks aus, welche die neuen Gebäude – ein Mehrzweckzentrum für die Gemeinde, ein Altenheim sowie einige Apartments für betreutes Wohnen – miteinander verbinden. Wenn die Bewohner eines Gebiets unaufhörlich die alte Inkunabel von Grund und Boden umschreiben, die so einem Palimpsest ähnelt, wie André Corboz einmal erklärte, dann war es in diesen beiden letzten Situationen erforderlich, eine zeitgenössische Geschichte zu «schreiben», ohne dabei respektlos vor dem Bestehenden zu sein.

Doch es waren andere Massstäbe und andere Dimensionen, die das berufliche Interesse der Architekten erregt haben. Ich denke dabei an die unterstützende Tätigkeit für die Bauherrschaft, die Architetti Tibiletti Associati im Laufe der letzten zehn Jahre mit Architekturwettbewerben und Auswahlverfahren entwickelt hat. In Wahrheit erscheint mir der Begriff «Unterstützung der Bauherrschaft» nicht generös gegenüber jemandem, der sich um diese Art Prozesse kümmert. Dies beschränkt sich nämlich nicht auf eine einfache technische Hilfestellung zur Umsetzung der Bedürfnisse des Auftraggebers, es handelt sich vielmehr darum, einen Ablauf zu «problematisieren», indem man den Zielsetzungen (die häufig die einer öffentlich-rechtlichen Körperschaft sind) Rechnung trägt und sich an die Teilnehmer der Ausschreibung wendet, die diese politischen, technischen und auch kulturellen Erfordernisse aufgreifen und in ihre Planungsvisionen einbeziehen müssen. Um eine Wettbewerbsausschreibung zu organisieren, mit den verschiedenen Akteuren (Politikern, Sachverständigen, Technikern und Bürgern) Gespräche zu führen, das Verfahren der Protagonisten zu verfolgen und zu bewerten, einen Prozess zu lenken, der sich in zeitlichen Etappen entwickelt, muss man über eine solide Kenntnis der «Kultur des Territoriums» und über gute Vermittlungs- und Kommunikationsfähigkeiten verfügen.

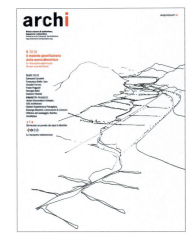

archi 6/2018, Das Planungsmodell des neuen Mendrisio
archi **6/2018, Planning model for the new Mendrisio**

Und die vom Büro Architetti Tibiletti Associati in diesen Jahren organisierten Verfahren sind zahlreich. Von den Architekturwettbewerben können wir das Langlaufzentrum von Campra anführen, während von den Parallelbeauftragungen die städtebauliche Entwicklung der Viertel Bosciorina und Quinta in Biasca sowie die des ehemaligen Schlachthofgeländes in Lugano zu erwähnen wären. Einige dieser Wettbewerbe haben auch besonders den landschaftlichen Massstab berührt. Zwei Massnahmen, welche die Stadt und den Luganersee einbezogen haben, verdienen es meiner Ansicht nach, in diesem Zusammenhang erwähnt zu werden: die Sanierung und Aufwertung des Seeufers in Paradiso und der Entwurf für die Seepromenade «Lungolago» für das Zentrum Luganos. Die erste Massnahme, die bereits umgesetzt wird, betrifft sozusagen eine «Randlage», wo fast keine Seepromenade existiert und sich einige schwerwiegende und komplexe Problemstellungen auftun, was das Verhältnis zwischen öffentlich und privat anbelangt. Hier mussten neue Wegführungen – auch mit Stegen, die auf den See hinausführen –, öffentliche Räume und neue Parks angelegt werden. Die zweite Massnahme – die Planung für Seepromenade und Zentrum in Lugano, die sich noch in der Entwicklungsphase befindet – betrifft ein Gebiet mit einer Bebauung aus der zweiten Hälfte des 19. und vom Beginn des 20. Jahrhunderts, das mit der wichtigen Frage nach der Mobilität verbunden ist und mit dem historischen Ortskern, der zu neuer Vitalität zurückfinden muss.

In diese landschaftliche und territoriale Logik gehört das von der Zeitschrift *archi* (6/2018) so bezeichnete «Planungsmodell des Neuen Mendrisio». Die Vorbereitung

centre, housing for the elderly and subsidized apartments. If, as André Corboz suggests, the inhabitants of a territory ceaselessly rewrite the old palimpsest-like incunabulum of the ground, then in the latter two projects, it was necessary to "write" a contemporary history without being disrespectful of what had already existed.

But other scales and dimensions have attracted the interest of our architects and their work. We refer to the client support activity that the Tibiletti Associati studio has been developing over the last ten years, with parallel design competitions and contracted studies. In reality, the term "client support" does not seem generous enough to describe those who deal with this type of procedure. In fact, it is not limited to mere technical assistance aimed at translating the client's needs, but is rather a matter of "problematizing" a process by taking the objectives into account (often those of a public body) and turning to the competition participants, who must apply and integrate these political, technical and also cultural needs into their design visions. To organise a competition, to enter into a dialogue with the various players (politicians, experts, technicians, citizens), to follow the designers' approach and enhance it, to guide a process that evolves over time through stages, requires a solid "culture of the territory" and good mediation and communication skills.

Numerous procedures have been organized by the studio over these years. Among the architectural competitions, we should mention the Nordic Ski Centre of Campra. Parallel study mandates include the urban development of the Boscorina and Quinta sectors in Biasca and the former abattoir/gas works in Locarno. Some of these competitions have involved the scale of the landscape in particular. In this context, it is worth mentioning two operations that involved the city and its lake: the redevelopment of the Lake Lugano shore in Paradiso and the project for the "Lungolago" and the "Lugano centro". The first, already under construction, is located, so to speak, in a "peripheral" situation, with an almost non-existent lake front and some major and complex problems regarding the relationship between public and private spaces. Here it was necessary to design new paths, even with walkways on the lake, new public spaces and new parks. The second procedure, Lungolago and Lugano centro, which is still under development, involves an area characterized by the presence of the quay built in the second half of the nineteenth and early twentieth centuries. In addition, there is the important question of mobility and the problem of a historical centre that must be revitalized.

And it is within this landscape and territorial logic that we find what the review *archi* (6/2018) called "the planning model of New Mendrisio". The preparation of this design required intense and productive discussion with the municipality's technicians and politicians. In this case, particularly on the valley floor, the traces of the past were obscured, in favour of a rapid and uncontrolled phase of territorialisation. But beneath the recent construction and transport infrastructures that occupy the plain, there is still a "hidden" landscape dimension waiting to be "discovered" and enhanced. Here it was necessary to consider historical, ecological and water constraints and reveal the palimpsest of the landscape and territory, transforming it into a matrix to work on. This is what the three multidisciplinary teams from three regions of the country have done. The groups participating in the competition "La città di Mendrisio un progetto territoriale" ("The city of Mendrisio, a territorial

dieses Prozederes erforderte eine intensive und nützliche Diskussion mit den Baubehörden und Politikern der Gemeinde. In diesem Fall waren vor allem in der Talsenke die Spuren der Vergangenheit zugunsten einer schnellen und unkontrollierten Phase der Territorialisierung verdunkelt. Doch unter den jüngeren Gebäuden und Verkehrsinfrastrukturen in der Ebene findet sich noch eine weitere «verborgene» landschaftliche Dimension, die nur darauf wartet, «entdeckt» und aufgewertet zu werden. Hier mussten bestehende historische und ökologische Bindungen sowie Wasserverbindungen berücksichtigt und der landschaftlich-territoriale Palimpsest zutage gefördert und in eine Matrix verwandelt werden, an der dann gearbeitet werden kann. Genauso haben es die drei interdisziplinären Teams, die aus drei Regionen des Landes stammen, gehandhabt. Die Gruppen, die an dem Wettbewerb «Die Stadt Mendrisio – ein territoriales Projekt» teilnahmen, haben Absichten und Ziele der Massnahme klar erfasst und es verstanden, eine aktualisierte Kenntnis des neuen Gemeindegebiets sowie bedeutende Entwürfe zur Verfügung zu stellen. Es sei ausserdem noch erwähnt, dass das Büro Tibiletti Associati im September 2020 ausgewählt wurde, Vorschläge für das wohl wichtigste städtebauliche Projekt dieser Jahre im Kanton Tessin, nämlich die Ausarbeitung des kommunalen Entwicklungsplans der Stadt Lugano, zu unterbreiten.

Als Fazit dieser kurzen Ausführungen meine ich behaupten zu können, dass Stefano Tibiletti und Catherine Gläser Tibiletti sich dazu entschieden, ihre Arbeit (vom Entwurf für ein einzelnes Haus bis hin zu einem Komplex städtischen Massstabs und zum Stadtplanungswettbewerb) auf einer «Intelligenz des Massstabs» aufzubauen. Sie verstehen es, die Dimensionen der Landschaft und des Territoriums zu berücksichtigen, die nicht als steriler Raum gedacht sind, den es zu vermessen und zu kartografieren gilt und in den man dann einfach ein Projekt stellt, sondern als einen identitätsgeladenen Ort sowie als Ergebnis einer Ablagerung von Geschichte und Erfahrungen.

project") have excellently understood the aims and objectives of the operation and have been able to provide fresh insight into the new municipal area and the highly interesting projects. Finally, we wish to add that in September 2020, the studio's proposals were selected to be included in what is undoubtedly the most important urban project in recent years in the Canton of Ticino, namely to develop the municipal master plan for the City of Lugano.

Bringing these brief notes to a close, I can confirm that Stefano Tibiletti and Catherine Gläser Tibiletti have decided to base their work (including single building designs, urban-scale complexes and urban planning competitions) on an "intelligence of scale" and know how to consider landscape and territorial dimensions that are not intended as aseptic spaces to measure, map and then merely design on top of, but as places that are filled with identity and the results of a sedimentation of history and experiences.

AUFSTOCKUNG EINES WOHNGEBÄUDES UM EINE ZWEIGESCHOSSIGE ATTIKA, VIA BUFFI, LUGANO

HEIGHTENING OF AN APARTMENT BUILDING WITH THE ADDITION OF A PENTHOUSE-DUPLEX, VIA BUFFI, LUGANO

Die Verdichtung und das Leben in der Stadt und zugleich der Umbau und die Aufstockung waren die Aufgabenstellungen dieses Projekts. Das bestehende, bescheiden dimensionierte Wohngebäude aus den 1930er-Jahren in einem Wohnviertel Luganos gegenüber dem Park der Universität bedurfte wesentlicher Sanierungs- und Umbauarbeiten. Im Rahmen dieser Planung beschloss der Eigentümer, durch Aufstockung eine Attikawohnung für seine persönliche Nutzung einzurichten. Durch den Umbau erhält das Gebäude neue Proportionen und eine Traufhöhe, die derjenigen der angrenzenden Häusern entspricht. Die Erhöhung der Fassaden führt die traditionellen architektonischen Charakteristiken des dahinterliegenden Gebäudes fort, bildet aber gleichzeitig einen andersartigen Abschluss mit einer durchgehenden Glasfassade aus, die im Vergleich zum bestehenden Gebäude zurückversetzt ist. Im vierten Geschoss, wo Eingangsbereich und Schlafzimmer untergebracht sind, wurde auf die Typologie der bestehenden Wohnungen in den entsprechenden Typologien der bestehenden Wohnungen zurückgegriffen. Das Wohngeschoss ist mit dem oberen Attikageschoss optisch durch eine zweigeschossige Treppe verbunden. Hier befinden sich der Wohnbereich sowie die Terrasse, die einen 360-Grad-Blick über die Dächer der Stadt eröffnet.

The design themes are aimed at improving the city's habitability and density, while at the same time restructuring and heightening the building. The existing apartment block, which is modest in size and was built in the 1930s opposite the university park in a residential area of Lugano, needed major renovation work. In addition to these measures, the owner decided to create a new penthouse apartment for personal use. Thus, the transformed building has new proportions with a height that is more suited to the neighbouring buildings. The heightening of the façades completes the traditional features of the building below, while also offering a different finish, with a continuous glass façade that is recessed from the exterior perimeter. The style of the fourth floor echoes that of the lower floor apartments; it accommodates the penthouse's entrance and sleeping area. The living room and terrace with a 360-degree view of the city's rooftops are situated on the top floor, which is visually connected by a double-height staircase.

Planung und Realisierung: 2005–2007
Bauherr: Familie Tibiletti
Bauleitung: Architetti Tibiletti Associati SA
Bauingenieur: Alfio Casanova SA, Lugano
Ingenieur HKLS: VTR Visani Rusconi Talleri SA, Taverne
Elektroingenieur: C&C Electric SA, Lugano
Inneneinrichtung: Lacasa interior design SA, Mendrisio

Design and construction: 2005/2007
Client: The Tibiletti Family
Works management: Architetti Tibiletti Associati SA
Civil engineering: Alfio Casanova SA, Lugano
HVAC and sanitary engineering: VTR Visani Rusconi Talleri SA, Taverne
Electrical engineering: C&C Electric SA, Lugano
Interiors: Lacasa interior design SA, Mendrisio

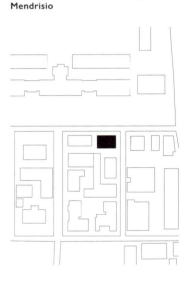

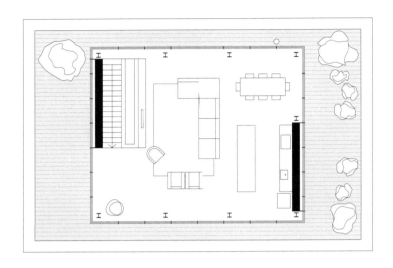

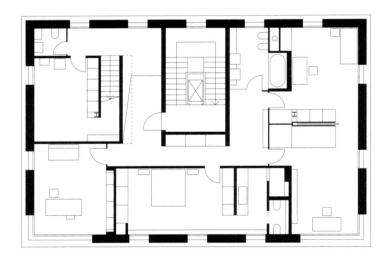

5 m

LABORE UND BÜROS AFLS, OLIVONE

in Zusammenarbeit mit Enrico Sassi Architetto, Lugano

AFLS LABORATORIES AND OFFICES, OLIVONE

Co-designer: Enrico Sassi Architetto, Lugano

Das Gebäude zeichnet sich durch zwei verschiedene Funktionen aus: Im Erdgeschoss befinden sich die Büroräume von AFLS sowie das Lehrlabor, im ersten Geschoss hingegen sind die kantonalen Labore für Gerichtstoxikologie und Bioanalytik untergebracht. Das Gebäude stellt eine Ergänzung des Komplexes Campus Gioventù und Sport Ticino dar und bildet einen neuen Baukörper, der den Freiraum zwischen den beiden bestehenden Militärkasernen begrenzt. Die Struktur besteht aus einem Holzrahmenbau mit Fertigdecken und -wänden und ruht auf sechs freigestellten Betonpfeilern. Braune, rohe, druckimprägnierte Längslatten aus Tannenholz bilden ihre Verkleidung. Das Wechselspiel von Zwischenräumen und den horizontalen Latten der Gebäudehülle dringt abends und nachts bei Dunkelheit das Licht aus dem Inneren nach draussen, sodass dieses Spiel die Leichtigkeit und Transparenz des Konstruktionssystems betont. Das Projekt reagiert auf drei wichtige Themen: den hohen Technologiegrad, der dem Labor zu eigen ist, zum Ausdruck bringen, einen Dialog zur Aufwertung des Umfelds suchen und schliesslich das Bild einer alpinen und zugleich zeitgenössischen Architektur vermitteln.

The building is distinguished by two different functions: the ground floor houses the AFLS offices and educational laboratory, while the first floor contains the cantonal laboratories for forensic toxicology and bio analysis. This new volume is the final building in the Gioventù + Sport Ticino Campus complex and forms a boundary along the empty space between the two existing military barracks. The structure consists of carpentry in wood with prefabricated foundations and walls, resting on six concrete pillars that separate the building from the ground. The cladding is made of fir slats with a rough finish, which is soaked in a brown colour through pressure painting. At night, the play between the horizontal solids and voids of the slats that form the building's shell emphasizes the lightness and transparency of the construction system. The design responds to three themes: to express the high degree of technology implicit in the concept of a laboratory, to seek a dialogue for the redevelopment of the area, and finally to offer an architectural image that is simultaneously alpine and contemporary.

Planung und Realisierung: 2005–2007
Bauherr: AFLS, Alpine Foundation for Life Sciences, Olivone
Bauleitung: Matteo Devittori
Bauingenieur: Enrico Prati, Biasca
Ingenieur HKLS: Studio ingegneria Zocchetti SA, Lugano
Elektroingenieur: C&C Electric SA, Lugano
Holzbauingenieur: Xilema, Bedano

Design and construction: 2005/2007
Client: AFLS, Alpine Foundation for Life Sciences, Olivone
Works management: Matteo Devittori
Civil engineering: Enrico Prati, Biasca
HVAC and sanitary engineering: Studio ingegneria Zocchetti SA, Lugano
Electrical engineering: C&C Electric SA, Lugano
Wood engineering: Xilema, Bedano

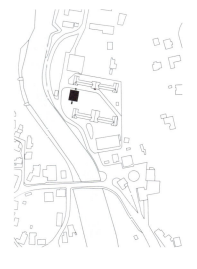

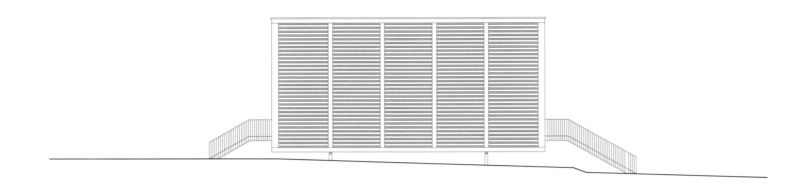
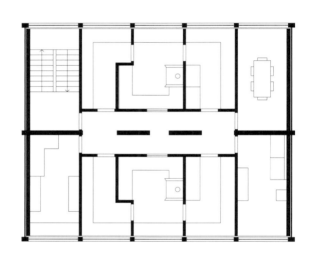
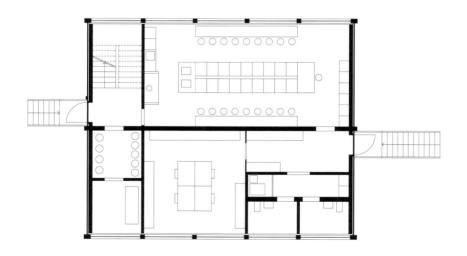

UMBAU UND ERWEITERUNG DES WOHNGEBÄUDES CASA DOPPIA, VIA DUFOUR, LUGANO

RESTRUCTURING AND EXPANSION OF THE "CASA DOPPIA" APARTMENT BUILDING, VIA DUFOUR, LUGANO

Der Entwurf entstand aus dem Erfordernis heraus, ein Wohngebäude vom Anfang des 20. Jahrhunderts vollständig zu renovieren und aufzustocken. Durch die ungewöhnliche Lage des Treppenhauses in einer Ecke des Gebäudes, bot sich genau dort, an der Südseite des Hauses, ein Erweiterungsbau an, sodass über das bestehende Treppenhaus alle zehn Wohnungen sowohl im Alt- als auch im Neubau erschlossen werden können. Die im neuen Bebauungsplan von der Strasse zurückversetzten Baulinie sowie die Begrenzung durch die Parkplätze auf dem Hinterhof haben Position und Dimension des neuen Baukörpers bestimmt. So entstand zur Via Dufour hin ein Atriumraum, der dem hinter dem bestehenden Wohnhaus bereits existierenden Hof entspricht. So wird ein Dialog zwischen den Vollformen und den Leerformen, die zusammen den Gesamtkomplex bilden, erzeugt. Dieses Wechselspiel stellt eine Dualität von Gegensätzen und Ergänzungen dar, wobei das einzelne Element, das vom jeweils anderen getrennt ist, keine geringere Kraft ausüben oder haben könnte.

The project arose from the need to entirely restructure and raise an early twentieth-century residential building. The staircase in the existing building, located in an unusual, lateral position, determined the new expansion towards the south and serves all ten apartments in the building and the new extension. The city's new development plan made it mandatory to set buildings back from the street, while the boundary created by parking lots towards the front courtyard determined the position and size of the newly added volume. A patio space was formed towards Via Dufour in correspondence with its existing counterpart towards the inside of the block. With the solid areas and voids creating a dialogue between the parts making up the whole, this alternation forms a duality of opposites and complementary elements, where the individual element, if separated from the other, could not exist or would be less powerful.

Planung und Realisierung: 2004–2009
Bauherr: privat
Landschaftsarchitektur: Studio Bürgi, Camorino
Bauleitung: Rolando Spadea und Marco Bondini Sagl, Lugano
Bauingenieur: Lurati Muttoni Partner SA, Mendrisio
Ingenieur HKLS: VTR Visani Rusconi Talleri SA, Taverne
Elektroingenieur: Elettroconsulenze Solcà SA, Lugano
Fassadeningenieur: Esoprogetti Sagl, Lugnao
Inneneinrichtung: Lacasa interior design SA, Mendrisio

Design and construction: 2004/2009
Client: Private
Landscape architect: Studio Bürgi, Camorino
Works management: Rolando Spadea e Marco Bondini Sagl, Lugano
Civil engineering: Lurati Muttoni Partner SA, Mendrisio
HVAC and sanitary engineering: VTR Visani Rusconi Talleri SA, Taverne
Electrical engineering: Elettroconsulenze Solcà SA, Lugano
Façade engineering: Esoprogetti Sagl, Lugano
Interiors: Lacasa interior design SA, Mendrisio

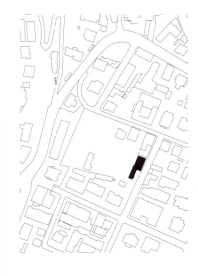

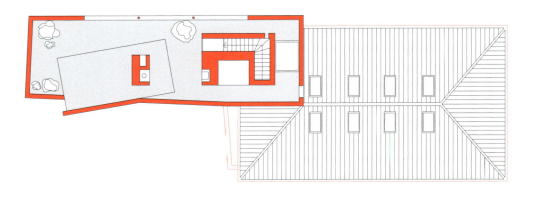
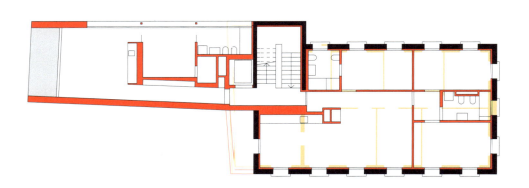
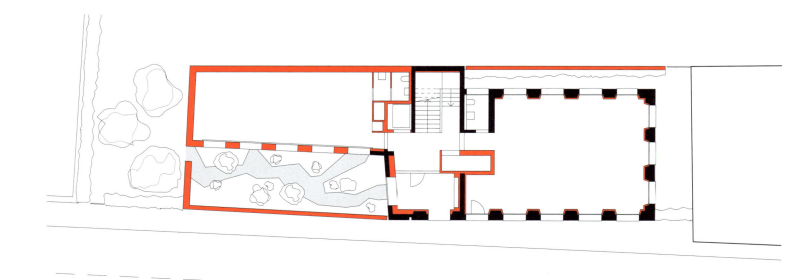

EINFAMILIENHAUS VILLA 101, VIA ALDESAGO, LUGANO

SINGLE-FAMILY HOME "VILLA 101", VIA ALDESAGO, LUGANO

Das Einfamilienhaus befindet sich an einem nach Südwesten orientierten steilen Berghang des Monte Brè; seine dominierende Lage erlaubt markante Panoramaausblicke auf den Luganersee. Die fantastische Landschaft, der Blick auf die darunterliegende Stadt und die Alpen in der Ferne bilden das idyllische Umfeld des Projekts. Die unregelmässige, längliche Form der engen, zwischen zwei Strassen unterschiedlicher Höhenniveaus gelegenen Parzelle sowie die Nähe zur Kirche von Aldesago bestimmten die Begrenzungen und die Geometrie der Architektur. Der Entwurf fügt sich in die bestehende Topografie mit fünf Geländeniveaus ein, doch lediglich die beiden Wohngeschosse treten aus dem Gelände hervor und werden vom Tal aus sichtbar. Im Zentrum des Tagesbereichs befindet sich der zweigeschossige Wohnbereich, seitlich von ihm liegen der Gästebereich sowie der Bereich des Bassins, während sich im Obergeschoss das Schlafzimmer und ein Arbeitsbereich befinden. Das Projekt ist in fünf Teile gegliedert, von denen drei die Hauptwohnbereiche und zwei die Servicebereiche umfassen. Sie werden durch vier himmelwärts und bergwärts gerichtete Oblichtfenster ausgezeichnet, die für einen zenitalen Lichteinfall sorgen und eine optische Verbindung zum Himmel und zum Berg hin entstehen lassen.

The single-family home is located on the slopes of Monte Brè and the steep terrain facing southwest towards Lake Lugano. The magnificent landscape, the view overlooking the city below and the Alps in the distance define the project's idyllic setting. The irregular, elongated shape of the plot, squeezed between two streets of different altitudes, and the proximity to the church of Aldesago dictate the limits and geometry of the design. It is integrated into the existing topography with five underground levels, but only the two inhabited levels emerge from the ground and overlook the valley. These two floors function as a living area at the centre, with the guest area and swimming pool on the sides. The upper floor houses the double-height living room, sleeping area and studio. The design is divided into five parts, three of which are main living spaces and two are service areas. Four skylights open towards the sky and the mountains, creating a visual bond with them and allowing overhead light to enter the building.

Planung und Realisierung: 2004–2009
Bauherr: privat
Landschaftsarchitektur: Studio Bürgi, Camorino
Bauleitung: Rolando Spadea und Marco Bondini Sagl, Lugano
Bauingenieur: Alfio Casanova, Lugano
Ingenieur HKLS: VRT Visani Rusconi Talleri SA, Taverne
Elektroingenieur: C&C Electric SA, Lugano
Inneneinrichtung: Lacasa interior design SA, Mendrisio

Design and construction: 2004/2009
Client: Private
Landscape architecture: Studio Bürgi, Camorino
Works management: Rolando Spadea e Marco Bondini Sagl, Lugano
Civil engineer: Alfio Casanova SA, Lugano
HVAC and sanitary engineering: VRT Visani Rusconi Talleri SA, Taverne
Electrical engineering: C&C Electric SA, Lugano
Interiors: Lacasa interior design SA, Mendrisio

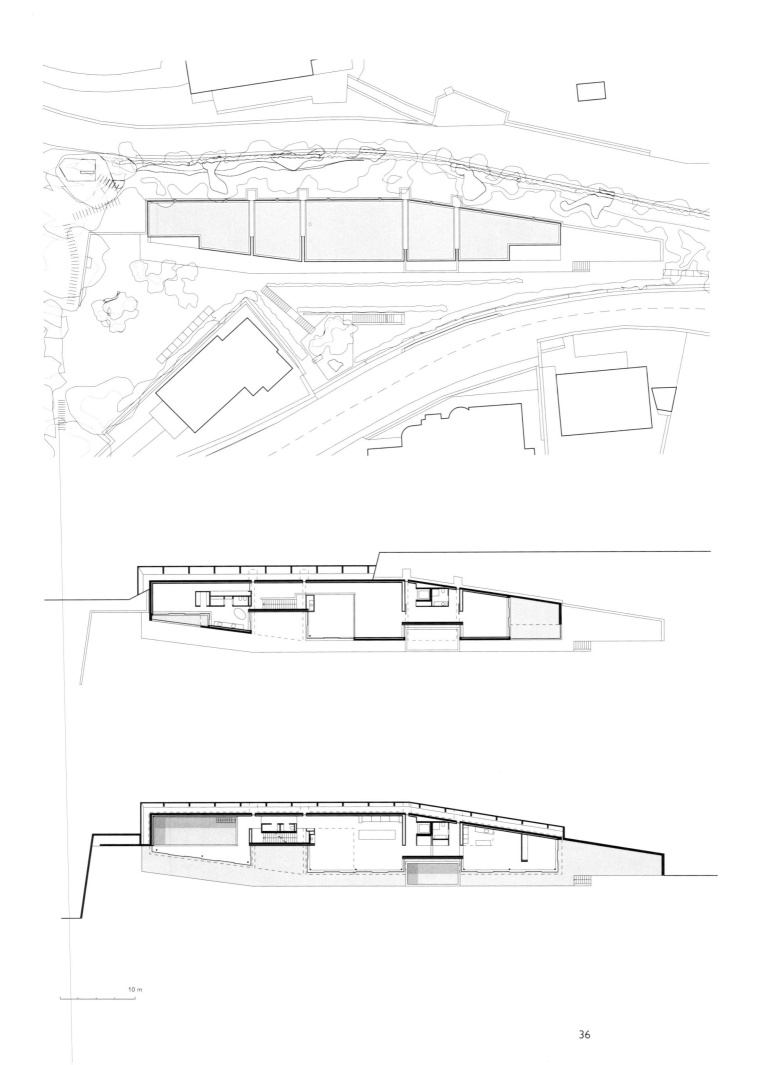

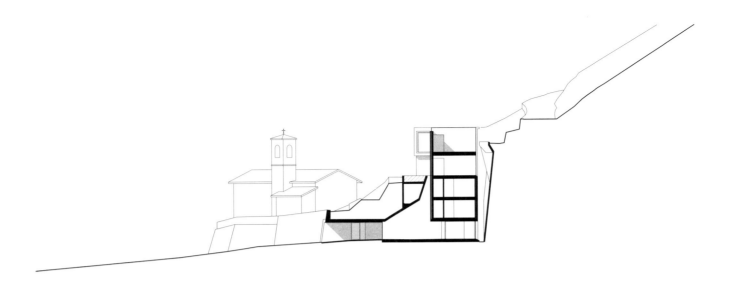
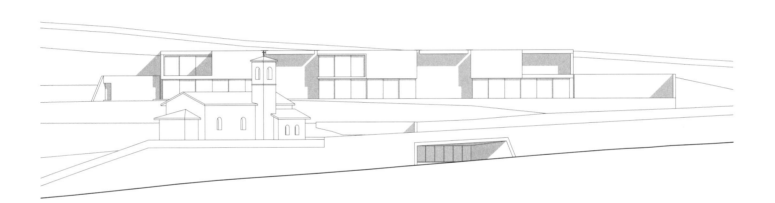
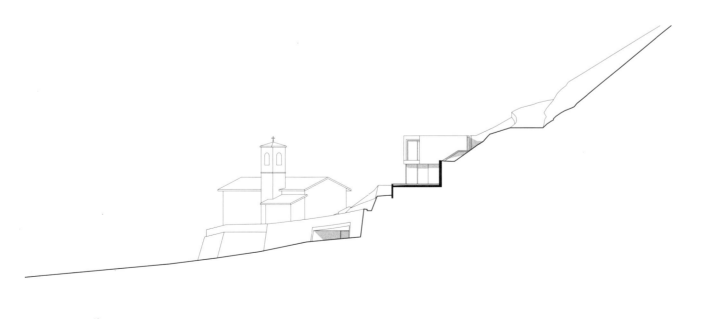

10 m

APARTMENTGEBÄUDE, VIA BELTRAMINA, LUGANO

APARTMENT BUILDING, VIA BELTRAMINA, LUGANO

Das Stadtquartier Molino Nuovo ist vom sozialen Wohnungsbau und von einer hohen städtischen Dichte geprägt. Der kompakte Baukörper mit seinen allseitig orientierten Fassaden besteht aus zwei symmetrisch gespiegelten Gebäudevolumina, wobei die Eingangsportale in enger Beziehung zum Zufahrts- und Gartenbereich stehen. Das Gebäude präsentiert sich als kompakter «durchlöcherter» Monolith, dessen Einschnitte nicht nur als Fensteröffnungen, sondern auch als Zugänge, Arkaden und Balkone fungieren. Das typologische Konzept basiert auf relativ kleinen kostengünstigen Wohnungen. Dabei stehen zwei unterschiedliche Typen zur Auswahl: 24 «Studios» und 12 «Lofts» mit Terrassen, alle vollständig möbliert, während sich im Erdgeschoss die Eingänge sowie Büroräume befinden. Die Besonderheit der Wohnungen besteht darin, dass sie sich dank des Spiels der versetzten Öffnungen jeweils voneinander unterscheiden. Deren Positionierung auf der Fassade folgt einem Schema, doch ihre Komposition ist frei, sodass ein abstrakter, pittoresker Eindruck entsteht. Durch die verschiedenen Positionen der Fenster eröffnen sich unterschiedliche Ausblicke und der Bewohner tritt in einen jeweils persönlichen und einzigartigen Dialog mit dem Quartier.

The district of Molino Nuovo is distinguished by its social housing and high population density and is mainly composed of apartment blocks. The design consists of two symmetrical halves that mirror each other and open on the ground floor towards the access road and the building's garden. The building appears as a compact "perforated and excavated" monolith, the perforations providing not only openings for windows, but also entrances, porticoes and terraces. This style was conceived for small low-cost apartment buildings. It offers two different types: 24 "studios" and 12 "lofts" with terraces, all fully furnished; the entrances and office spaces are situated on the ground floor. The way the openings are arranged makes each apartment different and unique. They are positioned along the façade according to a predefined module, in a free composition, creating an abstract impression, like a painting. The window positions provide different views towards the exterior, thereby establishing a personal and unique dialogue with the district.

Planung und Realisierung: 2009–2011
Bauherr: Hurrera SA, Lugano
Landschaftsarchitektur: Studio Bürgi, Camorino
Bauleitung: Rolando Spadea und Marco Bondini Sagl, Lugano
Bauingenieur: Lurati Muttoni Partner SA, Mendrisio
Ingenieur HKLS: Studio ingegneria Zocchetti SA, Lugano
Elektroingenieur: C&C Electric SA, Lugano
Inneneinrichtung: Salvioni Arredamenti, Lugano

Design and construction: 2009/2011
Client: Hurrera SA, Lugano
Landscape architecture: Studio Bürgi, Camorino
Works management: Rolando Spadea e Marco Bondini Sagl, Lugano
Civil engineering: Lurati Muttoni Partner SA, Mendrisio
HVAC and sanitary engineering: Studio ingegneria Zocchetti SA, Lugano
Electrical engineering: C&C Electric SA, Lugano
Interiors: Salvioni Arredamenti, Lugano

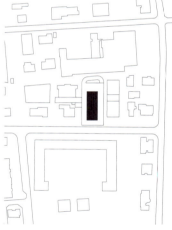

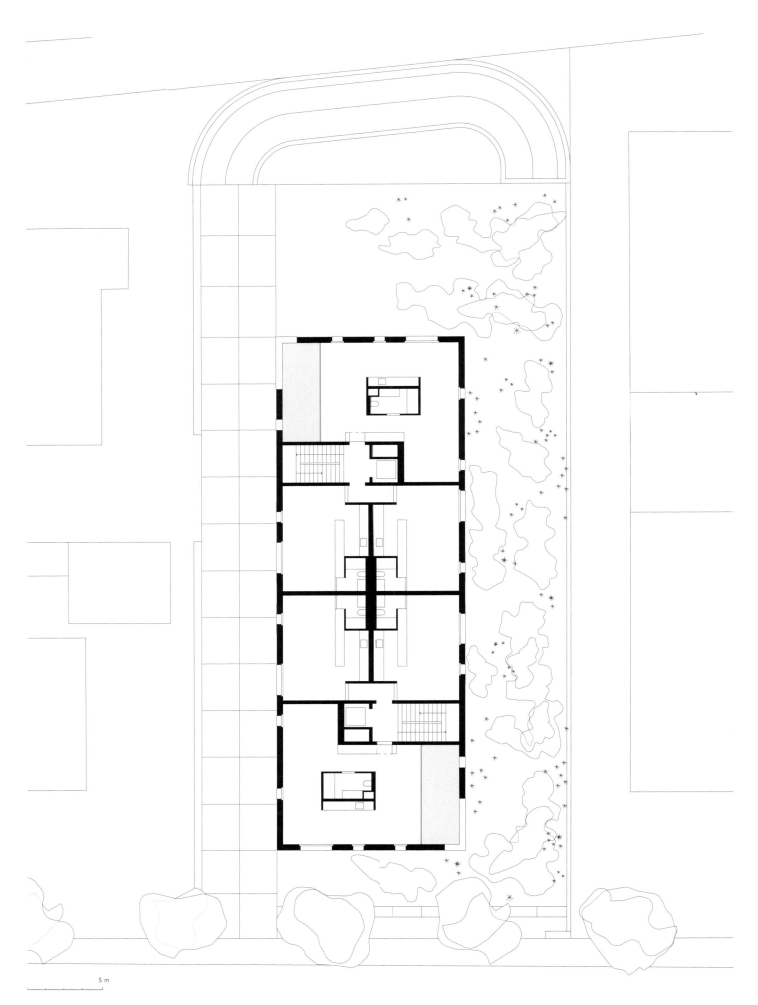

AUFSTOCKUNG UND UMBAU EINES WOHN- UND GESCHÄFTSGEBÄUDES, VICOLO NASSETTA, LUGANO

HEIGHTENING AND RESTRUCTURING OF A COMMERCIAL AND RESIDENTIAL BUILDING, VICOLO NASSETTA, LUGANO

Das Gebäude war ursprünglich ein reines Wohngebäude mit Eingang von der Via Nassa aus. Durch die Planung der Seepromenade und der damit verbundenen Öffnung der Riva Vela um das Jahr 1870 hatte sich das Verhältnis des Hauses zur Stadt verändert. Das Gebäude ist seither auch zum See hin ausgerichtet. Das Projekt modifiziert die Dachform, sodass durch die Aufstockung eine neue Mansardenwohnung entstanden ist. Baumassnahmen innerhalb des historischen Stadtkerns bedingen eine konservative Haltung. Gesimse, Dachtraufen und Dachgauben wurden rekonstruiert, um die Ergänzungen mit der bestehenden Architektur zu verweben und so ein neues Gleichgewicht zu schaffen. Das Innere wird zu einem einheitlichen Raum, in den die Serviceblöcke, losgelöst vom Dach, eingefügt sind und so vom Wohnbereich abgesonderte Vorräume bilden. Die Idee besteht darin, in der Wohnung die Kontinuität des Raums spüren zu lassen. Die Besonderheit der sichtbar belassenen Dachstruktur vermittelt trotz der geometrischen Abstraktion der Innenräume die Vorstellung, das Dach zu bewohnen: Ein emblematischer Platz zwischen Himmel und Erde, einst ein als Aufbewahrungsort genutzter Dachboden, ist nun zu einer der begehrtesten Wohnungen geworden, in der es sich wieder im historischen Zentrum leben lässt.

The existing building was originally an apartment block with access facing Via Nassa. The project on the lakefront, which opened the Riva Vela around 1870, changed the lakefront's relationship to the city, orientating it towards the lake as well. The project involves changing the shape of the roof, thereby heightening the building and creating a new penthouse apartment. Within the historical centre, any restructuring of buildings requires an approach of architectural conservation. Cornices, eaves and dormers were redesigned and revived to bring the whole together with a new balance. The interior is a single space into which the service blocks have been integrated, detached from the roof, creating the pertinent passageways for the inhabited spaces. The idea is to give the perception of spatial continuity from within the habitation. The unique features of the original structure, which is left exposed despite the geometric abstraction of the interior spaces, communicates the idea of inhabiting the rooftop: an emblematic place between heaven and earth. Once an attic space used for storage, it now becomes one of the more desirable apartments, returning to life in the historical centre.

Planung und Realisierung: 2009–2011
Bauherr: privat
Bauleitung Rolando Spadea und Marco Bondini Sagl, Lugano
Bauingenieur: Brenni Engineering SA, Mendrisio
Ingenieur HKLS: VRT Visani Rusconi Talleri SA, Taverne
Elektroingenieur: Elettroconsulenze Solcà SA, Lugano
Fassadeningenieur: Esoprogetti Sagl, Lugano
Inneneinrichtung: Lacasa interior design SA, Mendrisio

Design and construction: 2009/2011
Client: Private
Works management: Rolando Spadea e Marco Bondini Sagl, Lugano
Civil engineering: Brenni Engineering SA, Mendrisio
HVAC and sanitary engineering: VRT Visani Rusconi Talleri SA, Taverne
Electrical engineering: Elettroconsulenze Solcà SA, Lugano
Façade engineering: Esoprogetti Sagl, Lugano
Interiors: Lacasa interior design SA, Mendrisio

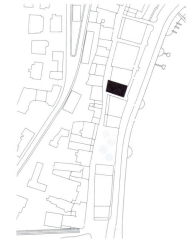

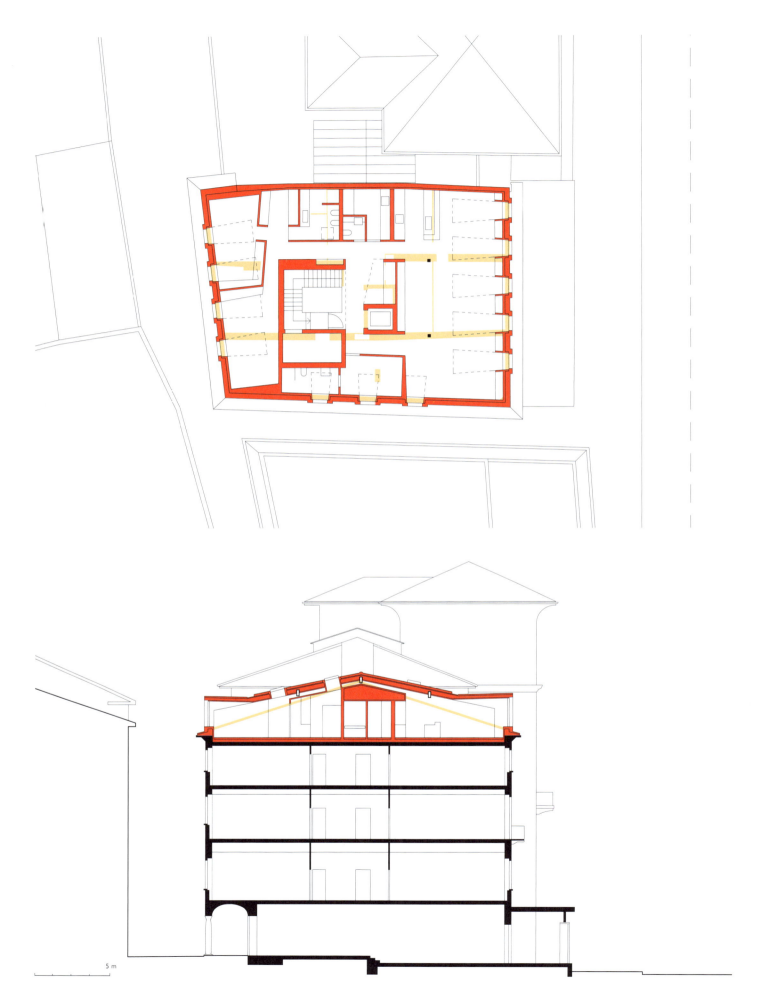

46

APARTMENTGEBÄUDE WESTSIDE 9, VIA SASSA, LUGANO

"WESTSIDE 9" APARTMENT BUILDING, VIA SASSA, LUGANO

Der Neubau steht in einem ruhigen, privilegierten Wohnquartier wenige Schritte vom Stadtzentrum Luganos entfernt, mit einer idealen Ausrichtung auf die Stadt und den See und einem schönen Panoramablick. Die Wohnungen sind entsprechend dieser Besonderheit entworfen. Sie öffnen sich über weiträumige Terrassen vor dem Wohnbereich nach Südosten. Das Projekt beinhaltet Wohnungen in verschiedenen Grössen mit individuellen luxuriösen Ausstattungen und mit Terrassen, Gärten sowie gemeinschaftlichen Sauna- und Fitnessräumen. Das typologische Konzept folgt der klassischen Raumaufteilung: einem bergwärts ausgerichteten Schlafbereich und einem talwärts orientierten Wohnbereich. Beide Teile wurden so gestaltet, dass sich in den einzelnen Räumen ihre Bedeutung und ihre Funktion widerspiegeln. So ist die Fassade des Schlafbereichs zur Zufahrtsstrasse hin ausgerichtet und die Räume zeichnen sich durch eine ruhige Orthogonalität aus, während der Wohnbereich bewegt gestaltet ist und sich zum See und zum Tal hin öffnet. Die verwendeten Materialien sind weisser Sichtbeton und pulverbeschichtetes Aluminium, das aussen sowohl bei den Fensterrahmen als auch bei den verschiebbaren Sonnenschutzscheiben zum Einsatz kommt. Der Garten gestaltet und komplettiert die Aussenräume und passt sich der bestehenden Topografie an.

The newly constructed building is located in a quiet and affluent area, a short distance from the centre of Lugano, with good exposure and panoramic views of the city and lake. The apartments are developed around these features and open to the southeast by way of large terraces leading from the living areas. The project involves the construction of nine apartments with varying sizes and customizable luxury finishes, terraces, gardens and communal sauna-fitness spaces. The typological concept is based on the classic subdivision into two parts: the bedroom area towards the hill and the living area positioned closer to the valley. The form of the two parts was designed to use the volumes to emphasize the differences in the interior spaces and their functions. The sleeping area faces the access road and is understated and orthogonal, while the living area is more dynamic and curved towards the lake and valley. The materials are white, fair-faced concrete and natural anodized aluminium for the window frames and sliding exterior sunscreen panels. The landscaped garden completes the outdoor spaces, adapting to the existing topography.

Planung und Realisierung: 2013–2014
Bauherr: privat
Bauleitung: Rolando Spadea und Marco Bondini Sagl, Lugano
Bauingenieur: Lurati Muttoni Partners, Mendrisio
Ingenieur HKLS: Studio ingegneria Zocchetti SA, Lugano
Elektroingenieur: Elettroconsulenze Solcà SA, Lugano
Fassadeningenieur: Esoprogetti Sagl, Lugano
Inneneinrichtung: Lacasa interior design SA, Mendrisio

Design and construction: 2013–2014
Client: Private
Works management: Rolando Spadea e Marco Bondini Sagl, Lugano
Civil engineering: Lurati Muttoni Partners, Mendrisio
HVAC and sanitary engineering: Studio ingegneria Zocchetti SA, Lugano
Electrical engineering: Elettroconsulenze Solcà SA, Lugano
Façade engineering: Esoprogetti Sagl, Lugano
Interiors: Lacasa interior design SA, Mendrisio

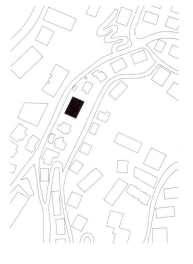

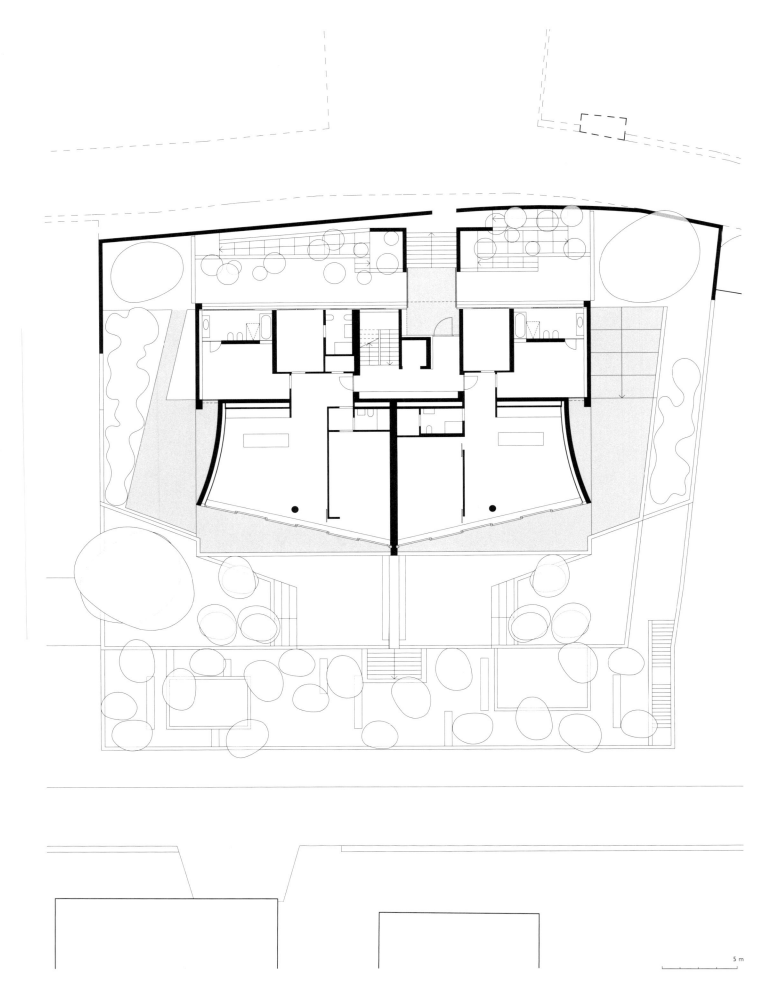

ERWEITERUNG UND UMBAU DES EHEMALIGEN RATHAUSES VON PREGASSONA ZU EINER GRUNDSCHULE UND GEMEINDEÄMTERN, LUGANO

EXTENSION AND CONVERSION OF THE FORMER PREGASSONA CITY HALL INTO AN ELEMENTARY SCHOOL AND MUNICIPAL OFFICES, LUGANO

Das ursprüngliche Rathaus von Pregassona wurde, zusammen mit der darunterliegenden Grundschule im Jahr 1960 von dem Architekten Alberto Tibiletti entworfen. 2004 war der Rathausbetrieb nach der Eingemeindung von Pregassona in die Stadt Lugano hinfällig. Daher beauftragte die Gemeinde das Büro Architetti Tibiletti Associati mit dessen Umbau und Erweiterung, um auf den wachsenden Bedarf an Unterrichtsräumen zu reagieren. Zusätzlich zu den Räumen der Grundschule in den unteren Geschossen wurden im Obergeschoss auch Räume zur Nutzung durch die Bewohner des neuen Quarties, ein Mehrzwecksaal sowie Räumlichkeiten für den «punto città» geschaffen. Die bestehende Tragstruktur besteht aus Stahlbetonpfeilern und Stahlbetonbalken, die über die äussere Wand aus Glasfenstern und Glastüren hinausragen. Die modulare Konstruktionstechnik und die freie Grundrissgestaltung ermöglichen es, mit dem Umbau und der Erweiterung die architektonische Charakteristika des ursprünglichen Gebäudes zu bewahren.

The original project for the City Hall of Pregassona, as well as the elementary school below, was designed by the architect Alberto Tibiletti in 1960. In 2004, after Pregassona was incorporated into the City of Lugano, it ceased functioning as the City Hall and the municipality asked the Architetti Tibiletti Associati studio to transform and expand it to meet the increased need for school spaces. In addition to the elementary school spaces, which are located on the lower levels, areas for use by the new district's inhabitants, a multipurpose room and "punto città" (municipal service) rooms are also located on the upper floor. The existing load-bearing structure is made up of reinforced concrete pillars and beams that extend outwards, protruding beyond the window and door frames. The modular construction technique of the open-plan structure makes it possible to reuse, transform and expand, while maintaining the architectural features of the original building.

Planung und Realisierung: 2011–2015
Bauherr: Stadt Lugano
Bauleitung: Bondini und Colombo Sagl, Lugano
Bauingenieur Studio d'ingegneria Lucini Cesare Sagl, Paradiso
Ingenieur HKLS: Studio ingegneria Zocchetti SA, Lugano
Elektroingenieur: Studio Elettro Ingegneria, Lugano
Fassadeningenieur: Esoprogetti Sagl, Lugano

Design and construction: 2011/2015
Client: City of Lugano
Works management: Bondini e Colombo Sagl, Lugano
Civil engineering: Studio d'ingegneria Lucini Cesare Sagl, Paradiso
HVAC and sanitary engineering: Studio ingegneria Zocchetti SA, Lugano
Electrical engineering: Studio Elettro Ingegneria, Lugano
Façade engineering: Esoprogetti Sagl, Lugano

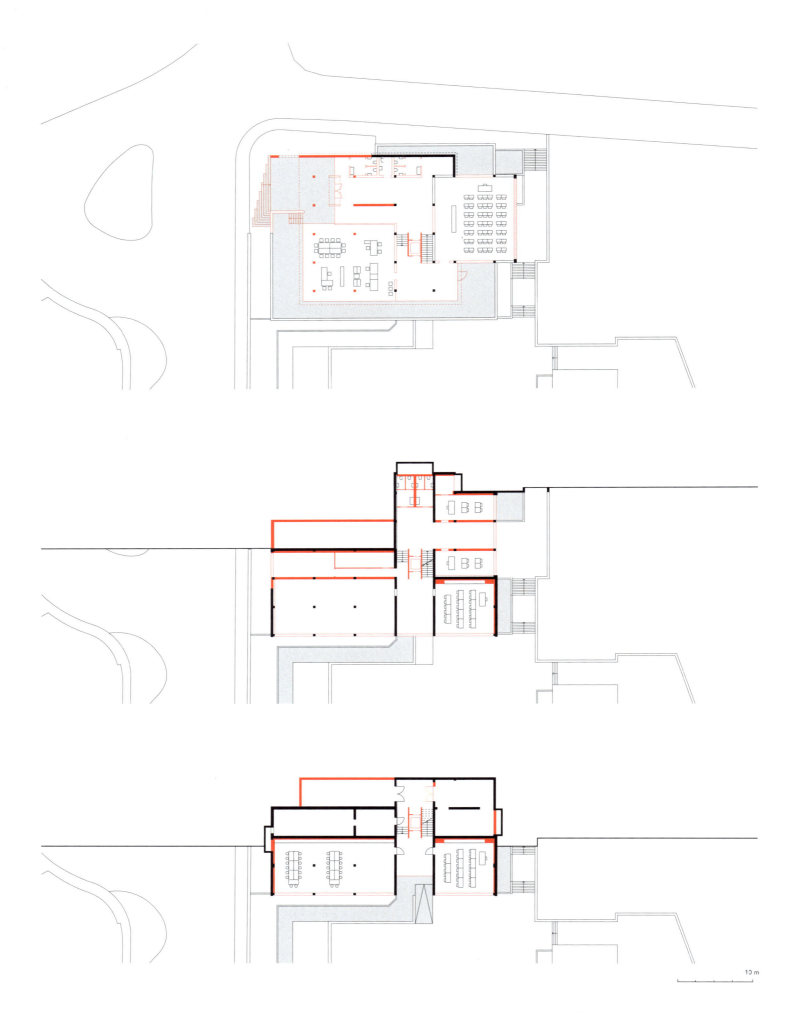

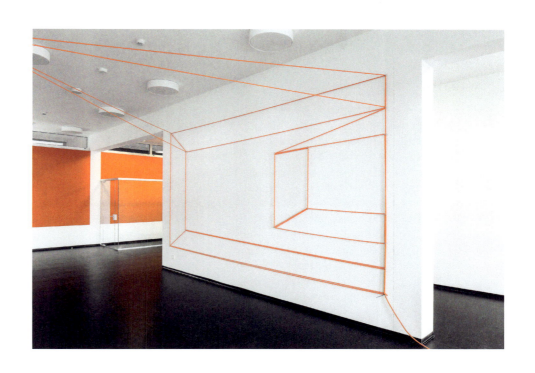

SENIORENRESIDENZ PARCO MOROSINI, AUFTRAG ZU EINER PARALLELSTUDIE: AUSWAHLENTWURF, VEZIA

"PARCO MOROSINI" RESIDENCE FOR SELF-SUFFICIENT SENIORS PARALLEL STUDY MANDATES: SELECTED PROJECT VEZIA

Nach Recherchen zum Projekt entstand der Vorschlag, ein neues Gebäude von qualitativ hohem Standard für nicht pflegebedürftige Senioren auf dem Privatgrundstück angrenzend an den Morosini-Park in Vezia zu errichten. Der Neubau setzt sich mit dem Park, seinem historischen und landschaftlichen Kontext und den Bestandsbauten wie etwa der Grabkapelle und dem Oratorium San Giuseppe und vor allem der Villa Negroni auseinander. Darüber hinaus ergänzt und schliesst er mit seinem langen, schmalen Baukörper die Umfassungsmauer des Morosini-Parks und dessen Grünanlagen. Die Zielsetzung war, die Verbindungen zwischen den einzelnen Teilen durch die Neudefinition der Grenzen der öffentlichen Grünanlagen zu verweben und zu verbessern sowie gleichzeitig die Nutzung des Parks zur Erholung der Bewohner der Gemeinde und der neuen Seniorenresidenz Parco Morosini neu zu beleben.

The aim of the project research is the design of a high quality new building for self-sufficient seniors, situated on private land adjacent to the Parco Morosini in Vezia. On one side, the new building faces the park and its historical, urban and landscape context, its pre-existing structures, such as the funeral chapel, the San Giuseppe oratory and particularly Villa Negroni. On the other side, with its long narrow volume, it completes and concludes the perimeter wall of the Parco Morosini and its green space. The aim is to reunite and improve the interconnections between the parts, by redefining the limits of the public green spaces, while at the same time revitalizing the recreational use of the park, which is available to local residents and users of the new "Parco Morosini" residence for self-sufficient seniors.

Planung und Realisierung: 2016
Bauherr: A.U.P.E. im Auftrag von A.I.L.A. Associazione Italiana Lugano Anziani
Landschaftsarchitektur: Stefan Rotzler BSLA, Zürich
Bauingenieur: Lurati Muttoni Partner SA, Mendrisio
Ingenieur HKLS: VRT Visani Rusconi Talleri SA, Taverne

Design and construction: 2016
Client: A.U.P.E. on behalf of A.I.L.A. Lugano Italian Seniors Association
Landscape architecture: Stefan Rotzler BSLA, Zürich
Civil engineering: Lurati Muttoni Partner SA, Mendrisio
HVAC and sanitary engineering: VRT Visani Rusconi Talleri SA, Taverne

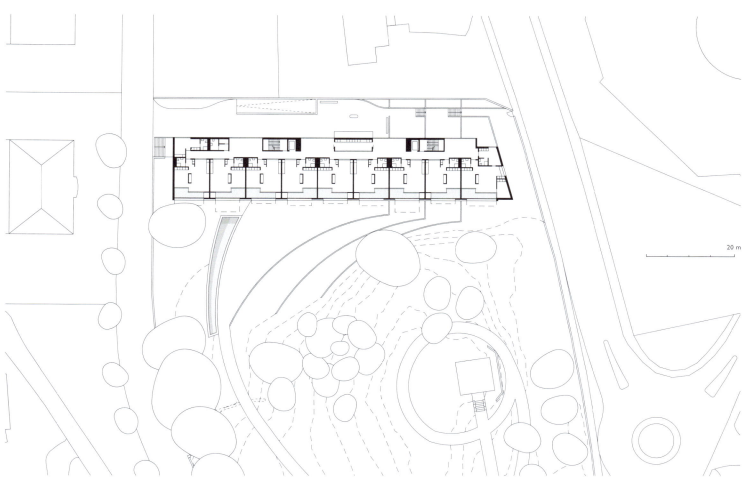

PARKHAUS OSPEDALE ITALIANO, VIA DEGLI ORTI, LUGANO

in Zusammenarbeit mit Remo Leuzinger Architetto, Lugano

OSPEDALE ITALIANO CAR PARK, VIA DEGLI ORTI, LUGANO

Co-designer: Remo Leuzinger Architetto, Lugano

Die 250 Parkplätze des Parkhauses sind für die Besucher und das Personal des Ospedale Italiano sowie für die Studenten und Professoren der benachbarten Universität bestimmt. Das transparente Erdgeschoss hat einen öffentlichen Charakter und ist mit einem Mehrzwecksaal und Geschäftsräumen ausgestattet. Daher hat das Gebäude nicht nur eine reine Parkhausfunktion, sondern unterliegt auch einer breit gefächerten Mischnutzung. Eine der Öffentlichkeit frei zugängliche zentrale Fussgängerpassage erschliesst die Räume, und ein Schacht versorgt das Gebäude über ein Oberlicht mit zenitalem Licht, das den Besucher überrascht und ihn in die höher gelegenen Stockwerke leitet. Die Ein- und Ausfahrten für Personenwagen erfolgen über gegenläufige Rampen, die an den Seiten positioniert sind, damit sie die öffentliche Nutzung des Erdgeschosses nicht beeinträchtigen. Die zu den höher gelegenen Ebenen auffahrenden Fahrzeuge werden auf der Suche nach Stellplätzen kreisförmig geleitet, und das Gleiche gilt für die Ausfahrt, wobei jegliches Kreuzen vermieden wird. Die Fassaden und die Dachverkleidung setzen sich aus einer Doppelstruktur aus Aluminiumdauben zusammen, die alternierend so angeordnet sind, dass Luft und Tageslicht Zugang finden, jedoch das Scheinwerferlicht der Autos nicht nach draussen dringen kann. Die Längslatten entsprechen in Ausmass und Typ den im Tessiner Bauwesen üblichen Latten, die nach den Tessiner Gipsern «stagge» genannt werden.

The 250 parking spaces in the car park are intended for visitors, hospital staff, students and professors from the nearby university. The ground floor is transparent, with a public character. It is used as a multipurpose space and has commercial areas, which is a distinguishing feature of the design with its mixed and diversified functions, in addition to vehicle parking. A public central pedestrian passage connects the spaces and the vertical ascents through a well with overhead light that surprises visitors, guiding them to the upper floors. Two-way ramps provide the entrance and exit for vehicles, arranged on the sides so as not to disturb the public use of the ground floor. Vehicle traffic going to the upper floors and looking for parking spaces follow a circular motion and the same applies to descending traffic, avoiding any intersection. The façades and roof cladding are composed of a double structure in aluminium slats arranged alternately to allow for the passage of air and natural light, but blocking the light from vehicle headlights. The slats are a size and type commonly found in Ticino construction, called "stagge" by Ticino plasterers.

Wettbewerb: 2004
Planung und Realisierung: 2014–2017
Bauherr: A.U.P.E. im Auftrag von A.I.L.A. Associazione Italiani di Lugaro per gli Anziani
Bauleitung: Konsortium A. Lepori SA und Garzoni SA, Lugano
Bauingenieur: Ingegneri Pedrazzini Guidotti Sagl, Lugano
Ingenieur HKLS: VRT Visani Rusconi Talleri SA, Taverne
Elektroingenieur: Elettroconsulenze Solcà SA, Lugano
Fassadeningenieur: Esoprogetti Sagl, Lugano

Competition: 2004
Design and construction: 2014/2017
Client: A.U.P.E. on behalf of A.I.L.A. Lugano Italian Seniors Association
Works management: Consortium: A. Lepori SA e Garzoni SA, Lugano
Civil engineering: Ingegneri Pedrazzini Guidotti Sagl, Lugano
HVAC and sanitary engineering: VRT Visani Rusconi Talleri SA, Taverne
Electrical engineering: Elettroconsulenze Solcà SA, Lugano
Façade engineering: Esoprogetti Sagl, Lugano

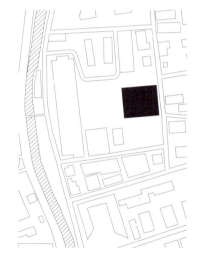

ARCHITETTI TIBILETTI ASSOCIATI

LA CHIAREZZA DELLA FIGURA ARCHITETTONICA
Alberto Caruso

Il progetto dell'architetto per la propria abitazione rivela sempre un aspetto autentico del suo pensiero. A volte si tratta di un aspetto intimo e profondo, difficilmente esprimibile nel confronto con il committente, oppure realizza, in forma contratta e simbolica, un'aspirazione architettonica che le occasioni professionali non hanno consentito di esprimere pienamente fino a quel momento.

La casa luganese di Stefano Tibiletti e Catherine Gläser Tibiletti è appena all'esterno della città compatta del '900, dove edifici isolati costruiti tra gli anni '30 e gli anni '50 del secolo scorso si alternano a giardini privati. La palazzina residenziale di quattro piani è stata sopralzata di un piano, con la stessa configurazione dei piani sottostanti. Sul tetto terrazzo è stato poi costruito un volume trasparente, destinato al grande spazio del soggiorno, che gode di una vista spettacolare della città – dalle montagne al lago – e che di notte diventa una lanterna luminosa, trasfigurando il carattere dell'edificio preesistente. (Fig. 1)

Oltre alla formazione culturale di Stefano e Catherine (entrambi hanno frequentato l'università di Ginevra, a quel tempo diretta da Bruno Reichlin) fondata sullo studio dei maestri del moderno, qui si rivela soprattutto la forte tensione verso l'urbanità che attraversa il loro mestiere. Quell'urbanità che ha caratterizzato la cultura architettonica ticinese del dopoguerra e che accomuna le opere degli architetti che hanno fatto conoscere il Ticino oltre i confini del continente. Architetti dalle poetiche e dai linguaggi differenti, uniti da un concetto condiviso: la convinzione che la città sia il modo più evoluto di abitare e il luogo sociale per eccellenza. La città come costruzione in continua trasformazione, terreno ideale per il mestiere. La città da riproporre come soluzione per il riscatto dei territori compromessi da espansioni disordinate e diffusione insediativa. La città come aspirazione, nel più dei casi avvilita dalla mancanza di occasioni professionali e dalla condizione politico-culturale che ha favorito il successo di modelli diversi e opposti di abitazione.

L'intensa e complessa relazione che le opere degli architetti ticinesi degli anni '70 intessono con il contesto naturale e con le tracce topografiche dei siti, deriva dall'elaborazione della nozione di città – e della tensione per realizzare la densità di relazioni propria della città – applicata al contesto del paesaggio naturale e delle aree scarsamente abitate.

Nel Bagno Pubblico di Bellinzona (Galfetti, Ruchat, Trümpy 1970), l'opera più eloquente di quegli anni, la passerella che attraversa l'insediamento in quota e collega la città al fiume è un gesto di urbanità senza precedenti e sottende una vera e propria idea di città. Il salto di scala stabilisce la piena appartenenza del Bagno Pubblico alla città, al suo sistema denso e storicamente stratificato di relazioni.

Negli anni '60 e '70 le piccole città ticinesi non offrivano abitazioni corrispondenti alla nuova domanda della giovane borghesia ticinese, formatasi in seguito allo sviluppo economico del dopoguerra. Il modello di abitazione unifamiliare extraurbano adottato dai nuovi ceti, magistralmente interpretato dai nuovi architetti, è stato negli anni successivi condiviso da tutti i ceti e, favorito dal credito e dalla politica urbanistica liberista, ha lentamente invaso il territorio dei fondivalle e le rive dei laghi. Tra le aspirazioni urbane della cultura architettonica e la realtà della condizione territoriale si è, quindi, formata una distanza crescente e problematica. Distanza che oggi si registra tra le proposte degli architetti colti e le strategie immobiliari dirette a soddisfare la domanda più diffusa. Il lavoro di Tibiletti Associati è segnato da queste aspirazioni. Hanno scelto di abitare in città e hanno costruito la loro casa sopra un'altra casa, con un gesto inequivocabile a favore della città, della densità e della socialità urbana.

Tra le opere realizzate a Lugano, Casa Doppia (Fig. 2) – costruita nel 2009 nello stesso quartiere della loro abitazione – è forse l'architettura che rappresenta nel modo più eloquente il loro atteggiamento progettuale. Il piccolo edificio novecentesco dall'aspetto severo e civile è stato ristrutturato e raddoppiato con un ampliamento moderno composto da un secondo volume. Il nuovo è un fabbricato dalla figura architettonica autonoma, e un unico collegamento verticale serve entrambe le unità abitative. La pianta dell'ampliamento, elementare e razionalissima, distribuisce un corpo di fabbrica dalla sezione minuta e scostata dall'allineamento stradale quel poco sufficiente a conferirgli indipendenza figurativa, sottolineata dai due piani in più rispetto al preesistente. Il fronte stradale è cieco, mentre i soggiorni si aprono su una serie sovrapposta di logge direzionate verso il centro della

Fig. 1 Sopraelevazione di uno stabile d'appartamenti in attico-duplex, Via Buffi Lugano

Fig. 2 Ristrutturazione e ampliamento dello stabile d'appartamenti "Casa Doppia", Via Doufur Lugano

città. La grande parete del fronte interno è tagliata in orizzontale da una fila serrata di Bandfenster, che richiamano in modo esplicito il linguaggio della tradizione razionalista mitteleuropea. Il tetto terrazzo è un belvedere sulla città, la cui funzione è esaltata dalla deformazione della superficie del fronte stradale, che apre la vista verso il lago. Oltre al richiamo all'architettura bianca degli anni '30, Casa Doppia rivela, nel trattamento delle superfici e nell'originale chiarezza della pianta, il segno della suggestione della nuova architettura iberica – che in quel periodo viveva un grande successo mediatico – frequentata anche per la vicinanza di Stefano a Manuel e Francisco Aires Mateus per i quali è stato assistente all'Accademia di Architettura di Mendrisio. La questione più rilevante indicata da Casa Doppia è l'atteggiamento nei confronti della preesistenza, è la cura con la quale gli architetti Tibiletti hanno trasformato il vecchio manufatto, il cui carattere architettonico non è stato manomesso, ma valorizzato dal nuovo fabbricato, che a sua volta non ha rinunciato all'affermazione della sua modernità.

Residenza Galleria è un'altra opera cittadina (*Fig. 3*), situata sul lungolago di Lugano. Anche qui un fabbricato d'epoca – dal fronte ornato in modo ordinato e silenzioso – viene ristrutturato e ampliato. Il sopralzo realizza un nuovo e vistoso coronamento che, costruito sopra l'aggetto di gronda, si sovrappone all'architettura preesistente senza lederne i rapporti compositivi. Livio Vacchini – presso il quale Stefano ha svolto la prima pratica professionale – sosteneva che negli edifici cittadini il ruolo del basamento della tripartizione classica dei fronti (basamento, fusto e coronamento) viene svolto dal suolo artificiale, elemento comune della situazione urbana, e che quindi la progettazione deve mirare alla cura della relazione tra il fusto e il coronamento e del rapporto del manufatto con il cielo. La sequenza di grandi finestre che, come una greca, concludono Residenza Galleria, le conferiscono una figura elegante, capace di competere – con un artificio architettonico semplice – con gli altri edifici del fronte, diversi dei quali esibiscono forme esagerate.

Fig. 3 Sopraelevazione e ristrutturazione di uno stabile commerciale ed abitativo, Vicolo Nassetta Lugano

Tra gli edifici cittadini, la casa di via Beltramina, sempre a Lugano, è un'altra prova di razionalità distributiva, dentro ad un involucro dalla morfologia diversa da quelle fino ad allora praticate. Situata sul bordo della strada, si confronta con l'imponente e composito fronte del grande edificio residenziale costruito da Campi e Pessina nel 1995 e reagisce con un monolite perfettamente parallelepipedo, scavato soltanto nello spigolo dell'ingresso. La geometria perfetta è bucata da numerose piccole aperture di tre formati distribuiti liberamente, in modo da non mettere in crisi la sua integrità. Il monolite forato è una figura spesso frequentata nello scenario architettonico internazionale. E' un'opera introversa, che non cerca relazioni importanti, affermando perentoriamente la sua distanza rispetto all'edificio di Campi e Pessina.

Questo edificio rivela con evidenza la predisposizione degli architetti Tibiletti ad un disinibito e controllato empirismo, alla capacità di organizzare incursioni eclettiche in spazi architettonici anche lontani dai luoghi della modernità ticinese, sempre riconducendo queste prove ad una geometria rigorosa e coerente, ad una razionalità che costituisce il fondale fisso del loro mestiere.

Fig. 4 Casa unifamiliare, Cureglia

Casa Cureglia del 2004 (*Fig. 4, 5*) è la prima opera nella quale gli architetti esprimono questo atteggiamento in modo chiaro e autorevole. I tre "tubi" – come li chiamava Livio Vacchini – sono posizionati sul terreno secondo tracciati leggermente angolati tra loro. Motivati da ragioni distributive e dalla relazione con il paesaggio, i diversi tracciati provocano spazi di relazione dall'effetto insospettato, che conferiscono alla piccola casa spazialità inconsuete. L'architettura iberica – la cui forza attrattiva è motivata dalla peculiarità di un "regionalismo critico" parallelo a quello ticinese – è una fonte d'ispirazione importante nel loro lavoro. Il portico di Casa Duplo, del 2004 (in collaborazione con E. Sassi), (*Fig. 6*) richiama la forma di quello dell'Università di Aveiro di Alvaro Siza (*Fig. 7*). Il maestro portoghese ha insegnato come alcuni controllati disallineamenti e lievi deformazioni dei tracciati possano sortire – come avviene nella Casa Cureglia – effetti spaziali importanti, sia nello spazio interno che nelle relazioni con il contesto.

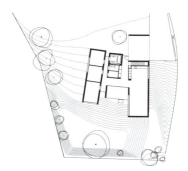

Fig. 5 Piano Terra, Casa unifamiliare, Cureglia

La pratica coltamente eclettica degli architetti Tibiletti li ha portati a sperimentare figure volumetriche tra loro diverse ed opposte, come nei disallineamenti di Casa Cureglia rispetto al monolite della casa di via Beltramina. Nella Villa 101 di Aldesago, il monolite si è frammentato in una sequenza di unità separate da lame di luce, offrendo al paesaggio il racconto compositivo degli otto piccoli volumi alternati tra pieni e vuoti, nei quali si articola la casa. L'intonaco bianco è diventato beton a vista, dalla superficie perfetta e raffinata come nella tradizione ticinese più celebrata. Il beton a vista conferisce, più di ogni altro materiale, la precisione e la solidità necessaria ad un'architettura che fonda la sua qualità sulla netta geometria del disegno. Una nettezza che non sarebbe realizzabile senza dettagli dettati da una spessa sapienza tecnica.

Anche l'autosilo dell'Ospedale Italiano è un monolite, realizzato con un involucro di profili metallici, ma in questo caso l'attacco al suolo è diventato uno strumento di relazione con la città. Il basamento,

ALBERTO CARUSO (TESTO)

(1945) architetto, diplomato al Politecnico di Milano, ha uno studio a Milano, associato con Elisabetta Mainardi. Ha pubblicato progetti su Casabella, Domus, Zodiac. E' membro associato della Federazione Architetti Svizzeri (FAS).
Nel 1996 e 1997 ha diretto *Rivista Tecnica*, nel 1998 ha fondato *Archi*, rivista della Società Ingegneri e Architetti svizzeri, che ha diretto fino al dicembre 2017. Nel 2008 ha pubblicato *La resistenza critica del moderno*, Tarmac Publishing Mendrisio.

CLAUDIO FERRATA (TESTO)

Claudio Ferrata è geografo, dottore di ricerca in Scienze economiche e sociali dell'Università di Ginevra ed opera nel campo della "Cultura del territorio". Ha insegnato presso il Liceo di Lugano 2 e la Facoltà di architettura del Politecnico di Torino. È autore di numerosi studi su questioni territoriali e paesaggistiche, il suo ultimo saggio dal titolo "Nelle pieghe del Mondo. Il paesaggio negli anni della Convezione europea" è stato recentemente pubblicato da Meltemi (2020).

Fig. 6 Casa unifamiliare, Cureglia

Fig. 7 Alvaro Siza Università, Aveiro

Fig. 8 Centro Macconi, Lugano

penetrato da un percorso pubblico passante, ospita spazi per riunioni e convegni, oltre agli accessi all'autosilo. L'infrastruttura per la mobilità non svolge soltanto il compito cui è principalmente destinato – il ricovero di automobili – ma è anche un elemento attivo di urbanità. Il mix funzionale promuove l'autosilo ad architettura urbana.

La padronanza con la quale gli architetti manipolano riferimenti diversi e sperimentano morfologie differenti è resa possibile dal loro saldo ancoraggio ai fondamenti della modernità ticinese. Il fronte del piccolo ampliamento de La Reparata, a Pregassona, è un vero e proprio omaggio all'asciutto linguaggio delle prime opere di Luigi Snozzi.

Stefano è figlio d'arte, il padre Alberto è un architetto della stessa generazione di Snozzi e di Vacchini, insieme al quale nel 1973–1975 ha progettato l'edificio Macconi (*Fig. 8*) nel centro di Lugano. Venticinque anni dopo, nel 2000, l'edificio è stato ampliato da Vacchini, insieme ad Alberto ed ai giovani Tibiletti, con un'addizione che rappresenta con eloquenza l'evoluzione dell'architettura ticinese. Alberto Tibiletti ha costruito molti edifici di rilievo, prove precise di cultura razionalista.

L'eclettismo colto degli architetti Tibiletti è un atteggiamento presente nella modernità ticinese, a cominciare dagli architetti della prima generazione. Rino Tami, Franco Ponti, Peppo Brivio, Augusto Jäggli, Alberto Camenzind hanno scoperto la modernità aderendo ai diversi linguaggi dei maestri europei dei primi decenni del '900. I maestri degli anni '60 e '70, quelli di Tendenzen, hanno guardato a Le Corbusier, a Mies, ad Aalto, a Kahn, traducendo le loro poetiche alla scala del paesaggio ticinese. I forti elementi, anche etici, che li accomunano non occultano mai le differenze dei loro linguaggi, cosicché non è possibile parlare di "scuola ticinese", come ormai tutti i critici convengono.

La cultura architettonica ticinese in questi ultimi anni sta vivendo una fase di ricerca, ed è diventata un laboratorio aperto a esperimenti in direzioni diverse. I protagonisti di questa fase sono gli "architetti colti", quelli che partecipano ai concorsi e li vincono realizzando le opere pubbliche, e che sono per lo più esclusi dal mercato dei professionisti di cui si servono i gruppi immobiliari speculativi. La ricerca di nuove strade è, nel lavoro di questi architetti, accompagnata dalla "resistenza" dei principi ereditati dai maestri.

La semplicità come esito finale di un percorso faticoso, il ricorso alla geometria e alla coerenza delle sue regole, il rifiuto dell'architettura come esibizione spettacolare, il rigore distributivo e la ricerca tecnica finalizzata all'esito spaziale.

Alcuni si propongono di aggiornare il pensiero di Luigi Snozzi, altri si dedicano ad una ricerca linguistica più larga e disinvolta, Ciò che li accomuna è comunque la motivazione razionale su cui deve essere fondata qualsiasi forma. L'architettura deve essere intelligibile. Deve essere possibile riconoscere i principi direttamente nelle sue forme, che devono essere comprensibili, realizzando in questo modo la dimensione civile del mestiere. La "comprensibilità" è una qualità del lavoro degli architetti Tibiletti, nei loro progetti la figura architettonica è elementare e comunicativa.

Tra gli ultimi lavori, il progetto del quartiere intergenerazionale di Coldrerio, nel Mendrisiotto, mostra un salto di scala e segnala che la condizione professionale sta lentamente mutando, offrendo occasioni progettuali più complesse, finalizzate a trasformare parti più vaste del territorio. Oltre alla nuova casa anziani, il concorso prevedeva spazi per attività sociali e aggregative, abitazioni e un riordino urbanistico degli spazi pubblici aperti: un progetto a scala urbana, per realizzare un sistema di relazioni spaziali che densifica l'area centrale del villaggio, disegnando un piccolo pezzo di città. L'intelligente proposta planivolumetrica prevede di adottare il tracciato della casa comunale e della scuola esistenti e di collocare il fabbricato principale nell'area verde retrostante stabilendo un preciso limite, anche di quota, tra il parco pubblico e la nuova area pedonale. La piazza così formata diventa il luogo di relazione tra le attività ospitate negli edifici nuovi ed esistenti.

La razionalità distributiva, finora sperimentata in diverse modalità all'interno degli edifici, qui viene ribaltata nella sistemazione degli spazi aperti. L'accento dell'invenzione progettuale è posto sui vuoti, che dominano il disegno e ne determinano la qualità. È così importante il concetto spaziale, che la composizione architettonica dei fronti passa in secondo piano: il raster di fasce orizzontali marcapiano e file verticali di serramenti – già sperimentato nella Residenza Parco Morosini – assolve il compito con economia espressiva.

La sfida che oggi impegna la ricerca – e che può aprire una vera stagione di rinnovamento per il "regionalismo critico" ticinese – è la progettazione a grande scala. L'inversione di tendenza della diffusione insediativa, il rafforzamento delle città per favorire il ritorno dei residenti dai territori periurbani, sono prospettive che possono essere realisticamente perseguite, se il contributo della cultura architettonica diventa protagonista. –

TRA LE SCALE DEL PAESAGGIO
Claudio Ferrata

Come parlare del lavoro degli Architetti Tibiletti Associati? Per un semplice motivo di competenza, vorrei tentare di inserire le realizzazioni dello studio in un contesto culturale e, in particolare, desidero mettere in relazione il lavoro architettonico con le nozioni di paesaggio, palinsesto e territorio. Pur avendo operato soprattutto in Ticino, e mantenendo solidi contatti con quella che impropriamente viene a volte chiamata la "scuola ticinese", la comune formazione ginevrina dei due architetti ha permesso loro di acquisire uno sguardo esterno. Mounir Ayoub recentemente, nell'editoriale del numero 23–24 della rivista svizzera *Tracés* (2017) si interrogava: Y a-t-il une école de Genève? La sua risposta era positiva. Quali sarebbero le sue caratteristiche? La "scuola ginevrina" si caratterizza per una attenzione alla dimensione urbanistica e paesaggistica, per un'attitudine critica e un interesse per il contesto sociale entro il quale si svolge la pratica dell'architetto. Gli insegnamenti di figure quali Bruno Reichlin, che allora dirigeva la scuola, Georges Descombes, Alain Léveillé, Riccardo Mariani, Giairo Daghini, Tita Carloni, Jaques Gubler e Bernardo Secchi, che Stefano Tibiletti e Catherine Gläser Tibiletti hanno avuto modo di seguire all'Ecole d'architecture de l'Université de Genève (EAUG), hanno certamente segnato la coppia. Essi hanno poi acquisto altre esperienze. Hanno collaborato con Secchi a Firenze e con Livio Vacchini a Locarno. Inoltre, la presenza per un certo periodo a Berlino di Stefano nello studio di Hans Kollhoff gli ha permesso di lavorare su grossi concorsi inerenti il rinnovo urbanistico della città nei primi anni che hanno fatto seguito alla caduta del muro.

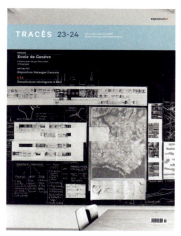

Tracés 23-24/2017, Ecole de Genève

Il sito è un punto denso di storia naturale e sociale, di segni e di valori e non deve essere visto in modo riduttivo come il semplice luogo fisico in cui si iscrive un progetto o come un semplice supporto. Non è solo lo spazio dove viene applicato un programma ma esso deve essere visto come una potenzialità. Penso sia corretto affermare che il lavoro di Architetti Tibiletti Associati, nelle sue varie forme, si iscrive in una logica di questo genere. Prendiamo il progetto per una abitazione sulle pendici del Monte Brè, ad Aldesago. La Villa 101 è collocata in una posizione che potremmo qualificare di "imbarazzante". Ha infatti davanti a sé quel "grand paysage" che comprende il golfo, le montagne circostanti e la città di Lugano. Come controllare questo paesaggio, il vicino e il lontano, l'orizzonte, senza produrre un'opera triviale? Il progetto permette di scoprire questo paesaggio gradualmente nel percorso che porta dall'accesso situato lungo la strada, passando attraverso una serie di spazi ipogei, sino all'arrivo nella dimora e all'uscita nel giardino. Il paesaggio così si si rivela. Spostiamoci ora in un contesto urbano, a Molino Nuovo, un quartiere popolare che ha ospitato la prima crescita della città di Lugano e che oggi è divenuto molto dinamico. Qui sorge la palazzina Via Beltramina 19 a+b che ospita piccoli appartamenti e *loft*. È inserita in un tessuto denso, dal parcellare ben leggibile, che viene occupato e completato dalla nuova edificazione in modo convincente. O ancora spostiamoci a Coldrerio, in una condizione di urbanità diffusa dove le tracce del passato agricolo della regione sono ancora parzialmente presenti in un contesto disordinato. Il progetto del Quartiere intergenerazionale in corso di costruzione, inserito in un comparto caratterizzato dalla presenza di alcuni edifici comunali, si qualifica per la presenza di spazi pubblici e giardini che collegano le nuove edificazioni, costituite da un centro polivalente per la comunità, una casa per anziani e alcuni appartamenti protetti. Se gli abitanti di un territorio riscrivono incessantemente il vecchio incunabolo del suolo che assomiglia a un palinsesto, come diceva André Corboz, in queste ultime due situazioni occorreva "scrivere" una storia contemporanea senza essere irrispettosi delle preesistenze.

Veduta aerea sul Mendrisiotto
Canton Ticino, Svizzera

Ma altre scale e altre dimensioni hanno suscitato l'interesse del lavoro dei nostri architetti. Stiamo pensando all'attività di aiuto alla committenza che lo studio Tibiletti Associati ha sviluppato nel corso degli ultimi dieci anni con concorsi di progettazione e mandati di studio paralleli. In realtà il termine "aiuto alla committenza" non mi pare generoso nei confronti di chi si occupa di questo genere di procedure. Infatti questo non si limita a una semplice assistenza tecnica volta a tradurre le esigenze del committente, si tratta piuttosto di "problematizzare" un percorso tenendo conto degli obiettivi (che sovente sono quelli di un ente pubblico) e rivolgendosi ai partecipanti alla gara, i quali devono assimilare e integrare nelle loro visioni progettuali queste esigenze politiche, tecniche e anche culturali. Per allestire un bando di concorso, dialogare con i vari attori (politici, esperti, tecnici, cittadini), seguire l'iter dei progettisti e valorizzarlo, guidare un processo che evolve nel tempo attraverso tappe, occorre disporre di una solida "cultura del territorio" e di buone capacità di mediazione e comunicazione.

archi 6/2018, il modello pianificatorio della nuova Mendrisio

E sono numerose le procedure allestite dallo studio in questi anni. Tra i concorsi di architettura possiamo citare il Centro di sci nordico di Campra, mentre per i mandati di studio parallelo ricordiamo lo sviluppo urbanistico dei comparti Boscorina e Quinta a Biasca e il comparto ex macello/ex gas a Locarno. Alcuni di questi concorsi hanno toccato in modo particolare la scala paesaggistica. Due operazioni che hanno coinvolto la città e il suo lago, a nostro avviso, meritano di essere evocate in questa sede: la riqualificazione della riva del lago di Lugano a Paradiso e il progetto per il "Lungolago" e "Lugano centro". La prima, già in fase di realizzazione, si colloca per così dire in una situazione "periferica", con un lungolago quasi inesistente e alcune importanti e complesse problematiche inerenti la relazione tra pubblico e privato. Qui occorreva immaginare nuovi percorsi, anche con delle passerelle sul lago, nuovi spazi pubblici e nuovi giardini. La seconda procedura, Lungolago e Lugano centro, ancora in corso di elaborazione, coinvolge un'area caratterizzata dalla presenza del *quai* edificato nella seconda metà dell'Ottocento e nei primi del Novecento a cui si aggiunge una importante questione legata alla mobilità e il problema di un centro storico che deve ritrovare una nuova vitalità.

Ed è in questa logica paesaggistica e territoriale che si iscrive quello che la rivista *archi* (6/2018) ha chiamato "il modello pianificatorio della Nuova Mendrisio". La preparazione di questo percorso ha richiesto una intensa e proficua discussione con i tecnici e con i politici del comune. In questo caso, soprattutto sul fondovalle le tracce del passato erano oscurate, a favore di una rapida e non controllata fase di territorializzazione. Ma sotto le recenti edificazioni e infrastrutture di trasporto che occupano la pianura, è ancora presente una dimensione paesaggistica "nascosta" e in attesa di essere "scoperta" e valorizzata. Qui occorreva considerare vincoli storici, ecologici e idrici e far emergere il palinsesto paesaggistico-territoriale, trasformandolo in una matrice sulla quale lavorare. È ciò che hanno fatto i tre team pluridisciplinari provenienti da tre regioni del paese. I gruppi partecipanti al concorso "La città di Mendrisio un progetto territoriale" hanno ben compreso intenti e obiettivi dell'operazione e hanno saputo mettere a disposizione una rinnovata conoscenza del nuovo territorio comunale e progetti di grande interesse. Aggiungiamo infine che in settembre 2020 lo Studio é stato scelto per portare le sue proposte all'interno di quello che é certamente il più importante Progetto urbanistico di questi anni nel Cantone Ticino, l'allestimento del Piano Direttore comunale della Città di Lugano.

Concludendo queste brevi note mi pare di poter affermare che Stefano Tibiletti e Catherine Gläser Tibiletti abbiano deciso di fondare il loro lavoro (dal progetto per il singolo edificio, al complesso a scala urbana, al concorso di urbanistica) su una "intelligenza di scala" e saputo considerare le dimensioni del paesaggio e del territorio, non intesi come uno spazio asettico da misurare e cartografare e sul quale poi semplicemente collocare un progetto, ma come un luogo carico di identità e risultato di una sedimentazione di storia e di esperienze.

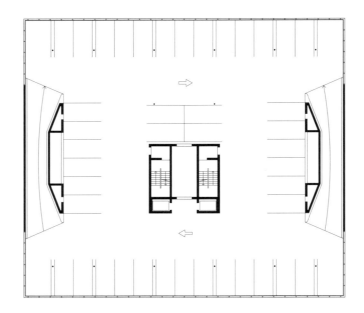
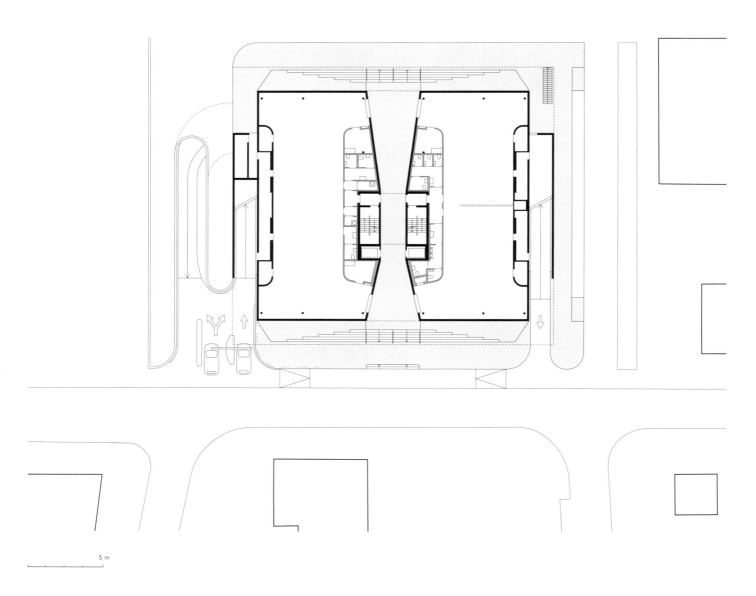

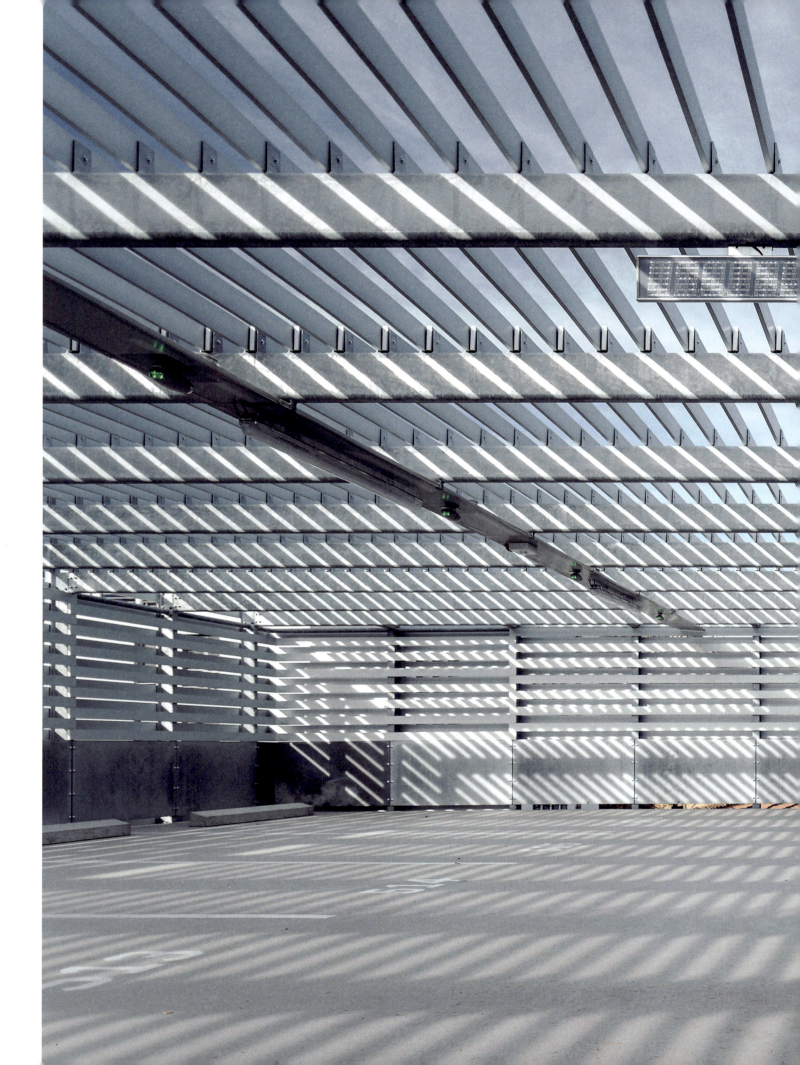

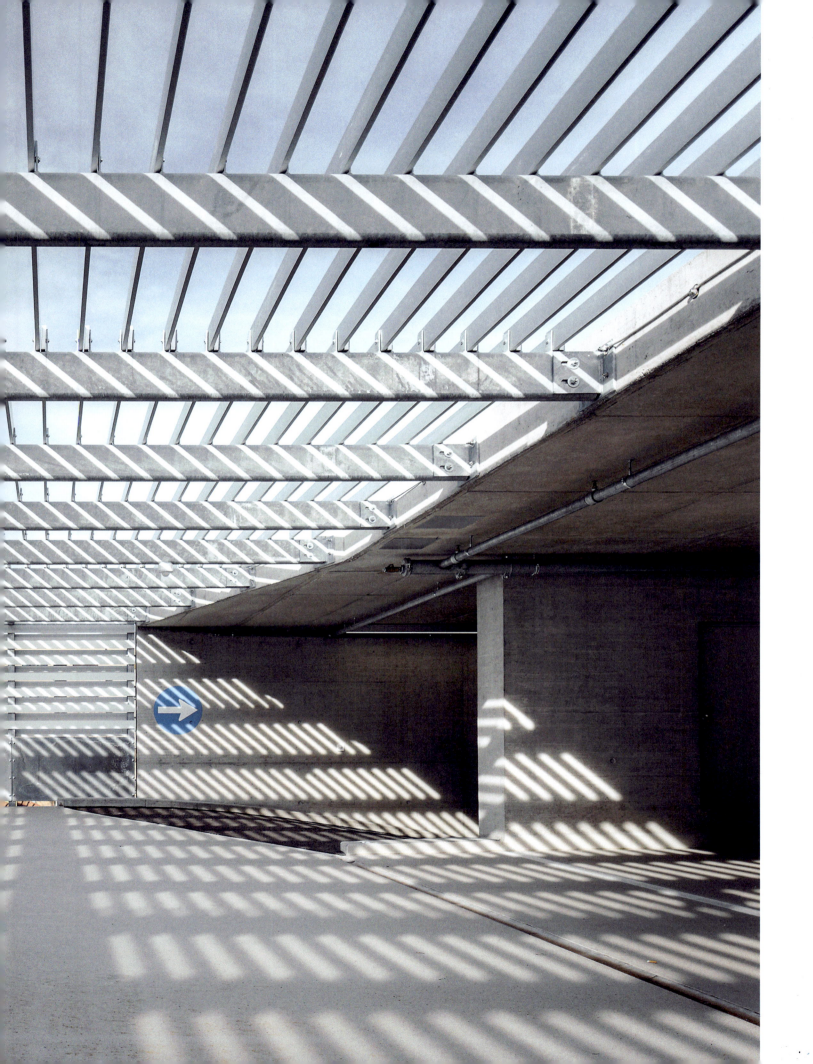

ERWEITERUNG DES CASALE LA REPARATA, LUGANO-PREGASSONA

"CASALE LA REPARATA" EXTENSION, PREGASSONA-LUGANO

Das Gebäude Casale la Reparata, erfuhr bereits 1994 Umbauarbeiten durch den Architekten Gianfranco Rossi. Die Planung für die Erweiterung sieht den Umbau der bestehenden, sich über drei unterschiedliche Ebenen erstreckenden Wohnung in zwei neue Apartments mit getrennten Eingängen vor, wobei eine Wohneinheit im Erdgeschoss liegt und die andere den ersten und zweiten Stock umfasst. Der neue Baukörper schliesst an den Bestandsbau mit einem verglasten, leichten und transparenten Verbindungsgang an, der sowohl das Atrium als auch den Garten im Erdgeschoss begrenzt, und sich unter Ausnutzung der Hanglage ins Gelände schmiegt. Der Neubau ist nach aussen von Sichtstahlbetonwänden umschlossen und öffnet sich nach innen durch grosse Glasscheiben zum neuen Garten hin. Alle Glasflächen sind mit verschiebbaren Sonnenschutzpaneelen aus Lochmetall versehen.

The "Casale la Reparata", the original building that provided the reference point, was enlarged in 1991–1994 by the architect Gianfranco Rossi. The expansion project therefore fits into a situation that is already multi-layered and calls for the transformation of the existing 1990s apartment, distributed over three distinct levels, into two new apartments with independent entrances: one on the ground floor and the other from the first to the second floor. The new third volume is joined to the existing one by means of a light, transparent glass connecting walkway, which joins the patio on one side. On the other, the ground-floor garden fits into the ground, making use of its slope. The new building is enclosed in reinforced concrete walls that face outwards. It opens inwardly into the new garden by way of large windows. All the glass surfaces have external sun blinds made of perforated and sliding metal panels.

Planung und Realisierung: 2016–2018
Bauherr: privat
Bauleitung: Bondini und Colombo Sagl, Lugano
Bauingenieur: Lurati Muttoni Partner SA, Mendrisio
Ingenieur HKLS: VRT Visani Rusconi Talleri SA, Taverne
Elektroingenieur: Elettroconsulenze Solcà SA, Lugano

Design and construction: 2016/2018
Client: Private
Works management: Bondini e Colombo Sagl, Lugano
Civil engineering: Lurati Muttoni Partner SA, Mendrisio
HVAC and sanitary engineering: VRT Visani Rusconi Talleri SA, Taverne
Electrical engineering: Elettroconsulenze Solcà SA, Lugano

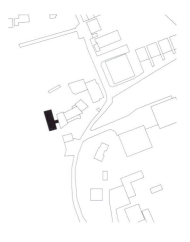

5 m

66

MEHRGENERATIONENQUARTIER PARCO SAN ROCCO, COLDRERIO

"PARCO SAN ROCCO" INTERGENERATIONAL DISTRICT, COLDRERIO

Das Wettbewerbsareal befindet sich in der Nähe eines der drei historischen Ortskerne von Coldrerio, nahe den öffentlichen Gebäuden und Schulbauten. Das Bauland liegt in einer grünen, zentralen und beliebten Zone, wenngleich diese derzeit keine eigene Identität und keinen Wiedererkennungswert aufweist. Das Projekt sieht die Ausbildung eines Gemeindetreffpunkts vor, der die synergetische Verbindung zwischen den neuen öffentlichen Gebäuden darstellt. Dieser Platz wird von der harmonischen Anordnung dreier Baukörper bestimmt – des Seniorenheims, eines Mehrzweckzentrums und einer Seniorenresidenz für Nichtpflegebedürftige –, die so konstruiert sind, dass sie sich in die städtebauliche Situation einfügen und die einzelnen Elemente verbinden. Die Zielsetzung besteht darin, eine Einheit zu komponieren, die den Ort aufwertet und einen Platz und einen Park schafft, die zur Verbesserung der Lebensqualität im Quartier beitragen sowie die gesellschaftliche Integration verschiedener Generationen fördern.

The site of the competition is located near one of the three historical centres of Coldrerio, characterized by some public and school buildings. The intervention area is located in a green, central and valuable area, even if at this moment it lacks identity and recognition. Some existing public and private buildings must be demolished for the construction of a new intergenerational district. The concept involves the design of a meeting space for the community, as well as connections between these new public buildings, creating asynergy between them. This meeting space is defined by the harmonious arrangement of three volumes, the home for the elderly, a multipurpose centre and a home for self-sufficient elderly people, built to be integrated into the urban situation by intertwining the parts. The goal is to recompose a whole to enhance the location, creating a square and a garden that contribute to improving the neighbourhood's quality of life, while promoting social and intergenerational integration.

Architekturwettbewerb, 1. Preis
Planung und Realisierung: seit 2016
Bauherr: Fondazione Casa San Rocco, Fondazione Ing. Giuseppe Croci-Solcà, Gemeinde Coldrerio
Landschaftsarchitektur: Stefan Rotzler BSLA+LAND, Zürich
Bauleitung: Direzione Lavori SA, Lugano
Bauingenieur: AF Toscano SA, Arbedo-Castione; Lurati Muttoni Partner SA, Mendrisio
Bauherrenvertretung: Comal.Ch, Morbio
Ingenieur HKLS: Rigozzi Engineering SA, Giubiasco
Elektroingenieur: Piona Engineering SA, Manno; Elettroconsulenze Solcà SA, Mendrisio
Fassadeningenieur: Feroplan Engineering AG, Chur
Lichtplanung: SPLD Swiss Professional Light Design, Paradiso

Architectural competition, 1st Prize
Design and construction: 2016/ongoing
Client: Casa San Rocco Foundation, Ing. Giuseppe Croci-Solcà Foundation, Coldrerio Municipal Hall
Landscape architecture: Stefan Rotzler BSLA LAND, Zurich
Works management: Direzione Lavori SA, Lugano
Civil engineering: AF Toscano SA, Arbedo-Castione; Lurati Muttoni Partner SA, Mendrisio
Client representation: Comal.Ch, Morbio
HVAC and sanitary engineering: Rigozzi Engineering SA, Giubiasco
Electrical engineer: Piona Engineering SA, Manno; Solcà SA electroconsultations, Mendrisio
Façade engineering: Feroplan Engineering AG, Chur
Lighting design: SPLD Swiss Professional Light Design, Paradiso

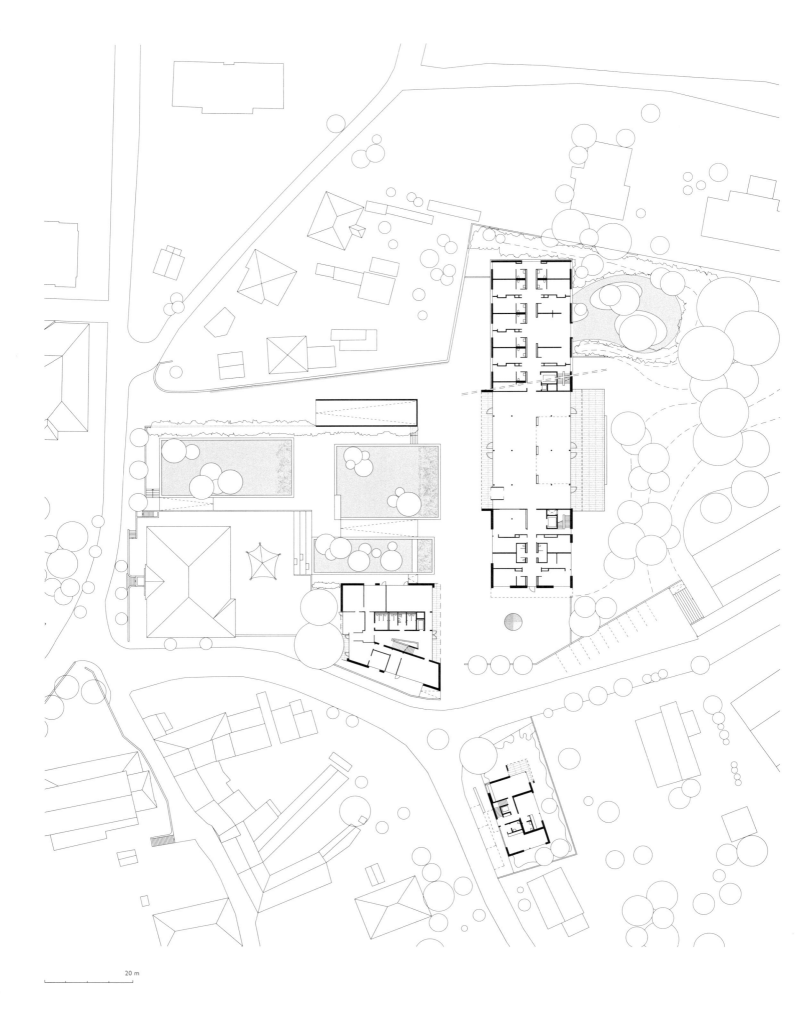

STEFANO TIBILETTI

1966	geboren in Lugano
1993	Abschluss des Architekturstudiums an der Architekturschule der Universität Genf, diplomierter Architekt EAUG, OTIA, SIA
1993–1994	berufliche Tätigkeit im Architekturbüro von Livio Vacchini in Locarno, bei Prof. Hans Kollhof in Berlin, DE, und bei Prof. Bernardo Secchi in Florenz, IT
1994–	zusammen mit dem Architekten Alberto Tibiletti Gesellschafter eines Architekturbüros in Lugano
1997–1999	berufliche Zusammenarbeit mit dem Architekten Livio Vacchini; Locarno
1998–2001	Redaktor der *Rivista Tecnica*
2001–2005	Mitarbeiter an der Accademia di Architettura in Mendrisio bei Prof. Aurelio Galfetti, den Professoren Manuel und Francisco Aires Mateus sowie bei Prof. Martin Boesch
2002–	Mitglied der Kommission für das historische Stadtzentrum von Lugano sowie die historischen Zentren der angegliederten Gemeinden
2004–	Redaktor der Zeitschrift Archi, des offiziellen Organs des Schweizerischen Ingenieur- und Architektenvereins (SIA), Regionalgruppe Tessin
2005–	Mitglied des Komitees ASPAN (Associazione svizzera per la pianificazione del territorio), des Schweizer Verbands für Raumplanung
2006–	Leitung des Architekturbüros Architetti Tibiletti Associati zusammen mit der Architektin Catherine Gläser Tibiletti
2010–	Mitglied des Redaktionskomitees von AS *Architettura Svizzera*
2015–	Mitglied der Regionalgruppe Tessin des SIA
2017–	Mitglied des Wettbewerbskomitees des SIA Tessin CCO
2017–	Mitglied der Kommission Coordinations Romande und TI CoRo
2018–	Mitglied der Kommission Tecnica Urbanistica Architettura CAT
2019–	Dozent an der Accademia di Architettura in Mendrisio USI-AAM für den Kurs «Dettagli Costruttivi 1»

CATHERINE GLÄSER TIBILETTI

1963	geboren in Genf
1983–1985	Studium der französischen Sprachwissenschaft an der Universität Genf
1991	Abschluss des Architekturstudiums an der Architekturschule der Universität Genf, diplomierte Architektin EAUG, OTIA, SIA
1991–1993	berufliche Tätigkeit in verschiedenen Architekturbüros in Genf, Berlin und Frankfurt am Main, DE
1994–	Zusammenarbeit mit dem Architekturbüro Architetti Tibiletti Associati
2006–	Leitung des Architekturbüros Architetti Tibiletti Associati zusammen mit Stefano Tibiletti
2007–	Mitglied des CSEA (Collège Suisse des Experts Architectes)
2015–	Mitglied der Berufsgruppe Architektur BGA innerhalb des SIA

MITARBEITENDE

aktuell	Tobias Biegger, Elisa Cherubini, Maddalena Corti, Benedetta De Rosa, Carlotta Fumagalli, Davide Gatti, Laura Martinez Dell'Olmo, Marco Torri
ehemalig	Luca Andina, Mehdi Aouabed, Reto Calignano, Géraldine Cappelletti, Elisabetta Clerici, Luca Coffari, Valeria Cosentini, Laura Ermanni, Ivan Iemma, Cristiana Lopes da Costa e Silva, Paola Marini, Matteo Marzi, Andrea Mazzucotelli, Armando Rathey, Ariane Scholer, Orsola Zannier
Praktikanten	Elias Aisama, Gabriel Dante, Olga Chernobrovkina, Christoph Florian Heitzmann, Stefanie Hitz, Stefano Pesenti, Ruben Semadeni, Chiara Scoca, Gabriela Trotta

STEFANO TIBILETTI

1966	Born in Lugano
1993	Graduated in Architecture at the Geneva University School of Architecture, Graduate of Architecture with EAUG / OTIA / SIA qualifications
1993–1994	Professional practice with the Livio Vacchini studio of architecture in Locarno, Professor Hans Kollhof in Berlin and Professor Bernardo Secchi in Florence
Since 1994	Partner of an architectural studio in Lugano together with Alberto Tibiletti
1997–1999	Worked in collaboration with architect Livio Vacchini
1998–2001	Editor of *Rivista Tecnica*
2001–2005	Collaborating architect at the Mendrisio Academy of Architecture with Professor Aurelio Galfetti, Professors Manuel and Francisco Aires Mateus and Professor Martin Boesch
Since 2002	Member of the Commission for the Historical Core of Lugano and the Merged Municipalities
Since 2004	Editor of *Archi* magazine, the official print media voice of S.I.A. Ticino
Since 2005	Member of the ASPAN Committee, Swiss Association for Spatial Planning
Since 2006	Head of the Architetti Tibiletti Associati studio with the architect Catherine Gläser Tibiletti
Since 2010	Member of the editorial board of *AS Architettura Svizzera*
Since 2015	Member of the SIA Ticino Committee
Since 2017	Member of the SIA Ticino CCO Competition Commission
Since 2017	Member of the Romande Coordinations Commission and TI CoRo
Since 2018	Member of the CAT Technical Commission for Urban Architecture
Since 2019	Lecturer at the Mendrisio Academy of Architecture USI-AAM for the course "Construction Details 1"

CATHERINE GLÄSER TIBILETTI

1963	Born in Geneva
1983–1985	Studied French language at the University of Geneva
1991	Graduated in Architecture from the Geneva University School of Architecture, Graduate of Architecture with EAUG / OTIA / SIA qualifications
1991–1993	Professional practice at various architectural firms in Geneva, Berlin and Frankfurt
Since 1994	Has worked with the Architetti Tibiletti Associati studio
Since 2006	Head of the Architetti Tibiletti Associati studio with the architect Stefano Tibiletti
Since 2007	Member of C.S.E.A. (Collège Suisse des Experts Architectes)
Since 2015	Member of the BGA Board (SIA)

EMPLOYEES

current	Tobias Biegger, Elisa Cherubini, Maddalena Corti, Benedetta De Rosa, Carlotta Fumagalli, Davide Gatti, Laura Martinez Dell'Olmo, Marco Torri
former	Luca Andina, Mehdi Aouabed, Reto Calignano, Géraldine Cappelletti, Elisabetta Clerici, Luca Coffari, Valeria Cosentini, Laura Ermanni, Ivan Iemma, Cristiana Lopes da Costa e Silva, Paola Marini, Matteo Marzi, Andrea Mazzucotelli, Armando Rathey, Ariane Scholer, Orsola Zannier
interns	Elias Aisama, Gabriel Dante, Olga Chernobrovkina, Christoph Florian Heitzmann, Stefanie Hitz, Stefano Pesenti, Ruben Semadeni, Chiara Scoca, Gabriela Trotta

WERKVERZEICHNIS
Auswahl Bauten, Projekte und Wettbewerbe

1995	Architekturwettbewerb, Planung Piazza Brocchi, Montagnola
1996	Architekturwettbewerb, Strassen- und Stadtplanung für den Ortskern von Canobbio zusammen mit den Architekten Silvia Regolati und Salvatore Lauria, 1. Preis
1997	Neubau Einfamilienhaus, Odogno
	Architekturwettbewerb, Ethnografisches Museum (Musée d'Ethnographie), Genf, zusammen mit den Architekten Silvia Regolati und Salvatore Lauria
1998	Architekturwettbewerb, Accademia d'Architettura, Mendrisio, zusammen mit den Architekten Silvia Regolati und Salvatore Lauria
1999	Neubau Einfamilienhaus, Manno
2000	Planungsstudie für den Bahnhofsbereich FFS, Lugano, zusammen mit der Architektengruppe Stazlu
	Neubau Einfamilienhaus Via Aldesago, Lugano
	Neubau Geschäfts- und Bürokomplex Centro Macconi, Lugano
	Architekturwettbewerb, Gestaltung der Seepromenade von Lugano
2001	Neubau Mehrzweckzentrum und Piazza Colombaro, Canobbio
	Architekturwettbewerb, Umbau der Kantonsbibliothek (Biblioteca cantonale), Lugano, zusammen mit dem Architekten Enrico Sassi
2002	Aufstockung des Hotels Federale, Lugano
	Architekturwettbewerb, neuer Kindergarten und Mehrzweckhalle, Comano
2003	Umbau einer Wohnung in der Via Aprica, Lugano-Besso, zusammen mit dem Architekten Enrico Sassi
	Garage und Garten für eine Einfamilienvilla, Lugano-Ruvigliana
	Architekturwettbewerb, Maison de la Paix, Genf, zusammen mit Aires Mateus, Lissabon (PT), 2. Abschnitt
	Architekturwettbewerb, neuer Kindergarten, Lugaggia
2004	Neubau Zweifamilienhaus, Cureglia, zusammen mit dem Architekten Enrico Sassi
	Neubau Einfamilienhaus, Cureglia
	Architekturwettbewerb, Kongress- und Ausstellungszentrum auf dem Gelände Campo Marzio Nord, Lugano
	Architekturwettbewerb, Ausbildungszentrum SSIC (Società Svizzera Impresari Costruttori), Gordola, 5. Preis
	Architekturwettbewerb, Wohngebäude der Pensionskasse für Angestellte der Stadt Lugano, 2. Preis
2005	Architekturwettbewerb, Schul- und Sportzentrum Traversee, Torricella-Taverne, 1. Preis
2007	Planung des Quartiers Ai piani, Brè, Lugano
	Aufstockung einer Duplex-Attika-Wohnung in der Via Buffi, Lugano
2009	Architekturwettbewerb, Parkhaus und Gestaltung des öffentlichen Raums, Colle di Sorengo
	geladener Architekturwettbewerb, neue kommunale Parkplätze, Carona
2010	Architekturwettbewerb, Kindergarten, Comano
	Aufstockung der Residenza Gemmo, Lugano
2011	Architekturwettbewerb, Campus der Universität Usi/Supsi, Lugano
	geladener Architekturwettbewerb, Credit Suisse, Quartiere Maghetti, Lugano, 2. Preis
	Architekturwettbewerb, Kindergarten und Mehrzweckhalle in Molino Nuovo, Lugano
	Umbau eines Dachgeschosses in der Via Cantu, Lugano
2012	Architekturwettbewerb, neues Gemeinde-, Wohn- und Geschäftshaus, Sorengo-Cortivallo, 1. Preis
	Architekturwettbewerb, Palazzo del Cinema, Locarno, zusammen mit dem Architekten Federico Fallavollita
2013	Neubau Einfamilienhaus, Caslano
2014	geladener Architekturwettbewerb, Mehrzweckzentrum Ingrado-Otaf, Bellinzona
	Auftrag einer Parallelstudie, Rione Madonnetta, Lugano
2015	Neubau Einfamilienhaus, Capriasca
	Neubau Mehrfamilienhaus, Capriasca
	Architekturwettbewerb, Erweiterung einer Grundschule mit Turnhalle, Tesserete
2016	Architekturwettbewerb, Kantonales Landwirtschaftsinstitut (Istituto Agrario Cantonale), Mezzana, zusammen mit den Architekten Giorgio Bello und Aydan Yurdakul, 4. Preis
2020	Umbau von Büros in der Via Volta 3/5, Lugano

Laufende Projekte
Neues Mehrgenerationenviertel von Coldrerio: Seniorenwohnstift, Mehrzweckzentrum, Seniorenwohnungen, Aussenanlagen von neuem Stadtpark und Stadtplatz
Umbau und Erweiterung des Büros von Architetti Tibiletti Associati in der Via Volta 3, Lugano
Gebäudemodernisierung und Adaption der Räume für neue Büros in der Via Balestra 10, Lugano
Adaption der Räume für das Istituto di sistemi e elettronica applicata in der Via Balestra 16, SUPSI, Lugano
Fassadensanierung des von den 1970er- bis 1975er-Jahren von den Architekten Alberto Tibiletti und Livio Vacchini erbauten und heute denkmalgeschützten Centro Macconi in der Via G. B. Pioda, Lugano
Umbau des Gebäudes «Coclemetro», Zürich-Schwamendingen
Umbau und Erweiterung eines Einfamilienhauses, Viganello
Entwurf: Variante des Bebauungsplans für den Bahnhof, Lugano
Wettbewerb: Öffentliche Räume und grosser Platz, Locarno
MSP: Auftrag zu einer Parallelstudie für das «Neue Lugano», Masterplan und kommunaler Entwicklungsplan

BIBLIOGRAFIE
Auswahl Bauten und Vorträge

2000	Alberto Caruso, Livio Vacchini e la città. In: *Archi* 5 (2000), S. 7–9.
2001	Architekten: Alberto Tibiletti und Stefano Tibiletti, Lugano; Livio Vacchini und Silvia Gmür mit Mauro Vanetti, Locarno-Basel, Edificio commerciale a Lugano TI, Ampliamento del Centro Macconi. In: *Rivista Tecnica* 11/12 (2001), S. 130–137.
2002	Agrandissement du «Centro Macconi». In: *AS Architettura Svizzera* 147 (2002), S. 21–24.
2003	Centro Macconi ampliamento uffici a Lugano del 2000, Casa unifamiliare Pickard ad Aldesago del 2000. In: *Katalog Premio SIA Ticino 2003*, 13.–28. Oktober 2003, S. 70.
	Maison Pickard. In: *AS Architettura Svizzera* 149 (2003), S. 25–28.
	Das Haus am Monte Brè. In: *Raum und Wohnen* 5 (2003), S. 52–63.
	Casa Manno, Tibiletti arquitectos. In: *Revista de Arquitectura e arte* 18 (2003), S. 48–53.

LIST OF WORKS
Selected buildings, projects and competitions

1995	Architecture competition, planning for Piazza Brocchi, Montagnola
1996	Architecture competition, road layout and urban plan of Canobbio nucleus, Co-authors: Architects S. Regolati and S. Lauria; 1st Prize
1997	Single-family dwelling, Odogno
	Architecture competition, Musée d'Ethnographie, Geneva, co-authors: Architects S. Regolati and S. Lauria
1998	Architecture competition, Academy of Architecture, Mendrisio, co-authors: Arch. S. Regolati and S. Lauria
1999	Single-family dwelling, Manno
2000	Planning study, FFS state railway station area, Lugano, co-authors: Gruppo Architetti Stazlu
	Single-family dwelling on Via Aldesago, Lugano
	"Centro Macconi" commercial building and offices, Lugano
	Architecture competition, reorganization of the Lugano lakefront
2001	Multipurpose centre and Piazza Colombaro, Canobbio
	Architecture competition, restructuring of the Cantonal Library, Lugano, co-author: Architect E. Sassi
2002	Hotel heightening, Albergo Federale, Lugano
	Architecture competition, new nursery school and multi-purpose room, Comano
2003	Restructuring of an apartment on Via Aprica, Lugano-Besso, co-author: Architect E. Sassi
	Garage and garden for a single-family villa, Lugano-Ruvigliana
	Architecture competition, Maison de la Paix, Geneva, co-authors: Architects F. and M. Aires-Mateus; 2nd phase
	Architecture competition, new nursery school, Lugaggia
2004	Duplex two-family dwelling, Cureglia, co-author: Architect E. Sassi
	Single-family dwelling, Cureglia
	Architecture competition, congress-exhibition centre in the northern Campo Marzio area, Lugano
	Architecture competition, SSIC Vocational Education Centre, Gordola; 5th Prize
	Architecture competition, residential building for the Employee Pension Fund for the city of Lugano; 2nd Prize
2005	Architecture competition, "Traversee" School and Sports Centre, Torricella-Taverne; 1st Prize
2007	"Ai piani" district plan, Lugano Brè
	Heightening of penthouse-duplex on Via Buffi, Lugano
2009	Architecture competition, car park building and public spatial organization, Colle di Sorengo
	Invitation architecture competition, new municipal parking spaces, Carona
2010	Architecture competition, nursery school, Comano
	Residence heightening, Residenza Gemmo, Lugano
2011	Architecture competition, Usi-Supsi Campus, Lugano
	Invitation architecture competition, Credit Suisse Maghetti district, Lugano; 2nd Prize
	Architecture competition, nursery school and multi-purpose room in Molino Nuovo, Lugano
	Penthouse renovation on Via Cantu, Lugano
2012	Architecture competition, new civic and residential/commercial centre, Sorengo-Cortivallo, 1st Prize
	Architecture competition, Palazzo del Cinema, Locarno, co-author: Architect F. Fallavollita
2013	Single-family dwelling, Caslano
2014	Invitation architecture competition, Ingrade-Otaf multi-purpose centre, Bellinzona
	Parallel study mandate, Rione (district) Madonnetta, Lugano
2015	Single-family dwelling, Capriasca
	Multi-family dwelling, Capriasca
	Architecture competition, elementary school and extension with gym, Tesserete
2016	Architecture competition, Cantonal Agricultural Institute, Mezzana, co-authors: Architects. G. Bello / A. Yurdakul; 4th Prize

Current projects
New intergenerational district of Coldrerio: Residence for the elderly, multipurpose centre, apartments for the elderly, exterior redesigning of the new urban park and square
Renovation and expansion of the Studio Architetti Tibiletti Associati at Via Volta 3, Lugano
Modernisation of the building and conversion of spaces for new offices at Via Balestra 10, Lugano
Adaptation of spaces for systems and applied electronics at Via Balestra 16, SUPSI, Lugano
Renovation of the façades of the Centro Macconi, built in 1970–75 by the architects Alberto Tibiletti and Livio Vacchini, and heritage-listed, on Via G.B. Pioda, Lugano
Renovation of the "Coclemetro" building in Zurich/Schwamendingen
Renovation and extension of a single-family villa in Viganello
Project: Variant of the master plan for Lugano Station
Competition: Public spaces and Piazza Grande, Locarno
MSP: Parallel study mandate for Nuova Lugano, master plan and municipal directorate plan

BIBLIOGRAPHY
Selected Publications and Conferences

2000	A. Caruso, "Livio Vacchini e la città". In: *Archi*, October, Issue no. 5, p. 7–9
2001	Architects: Alberto Tibiletti and Stefano Tibiletti, Lugano; Livio Vacchini and Silvia Gmür with Mauro Vanetti, Locarno-Basel "Edificio commerciale a Lugano TI, Ampliamento del Centro Macconi". In: *Rivista Tecnica*, September, Issue no. 11/12, p. 130–137
2002	"Agrandissement du Centro Macconi". In: *AS Architettura Svizzera*, December, Issue no. 147, p. 21–24
2003	"Centro Macconi ampliamento uffici a Lugano del 2000, Casa unifamiliare Pickard ad Aldesago del 2000". In: *SIA Ticino 2003 Award Catalogue*, 13–28 October, p. 70
	"Maison Pickard". In: *AS Architettura Svizzera*, June, Issue no. 149, p. 25–28
2003	"Das Haus am Monte Brè". In: *Raum und Wohnen*, May/June, Issue no. 5, p. 52–63
	"Casa Manno, Tibiletti arquitectos". In: *Revista de Arquitectura e Arte*, March/April, Issue no. 18, p. 48–53
2004	S. Tibiletti and E. Sassi, "Casa Duplo a Cureglia". In: *Archi*, May/June, Issue no. 3, p. 34–37
2005	StazLu Architects Group, "Area della stazione FFS, Lugano, Studio Pianificatorio". In: *Rivista Tecnica*, February, Issue no. 17, p. 80–93

2004	Stefano Tibiletti und Enrico Sassi, Casa Duplo a Cureglia. In: *Archi* 3 (2004), S. 34–37.
2005	Gruppo Architetti StazLu, Area della stazione FFS, Lugano, Studio Pianificatorio. In: *Rivista Tecnica* 17 (2005), S. 80–93.
	Tibiletti Associati, Lofts a Lugano. In: *Archi* 4 (2005), S. 40–41.
	Stefano Tibiletti, La stazione di Lugano. In: *Archi* 3 (2005), S. 28–34.
	Giornata svizzera dell'energia. Casa Duplo, (Vortrag), Accademia di architettura Mendrisio, 2005.
2006	Mehrfamilienhaus Casa Duplo. In: *AS Architettura Svizzera* 160 (2006), S. 39–40.
2007	Tibiletti Associati, Casa a Cureglia. In: *Archi* 1 (2007), S. 34–37.
	Casa a Cureglia del 2002–2004. In: *Katalog Premio SIA Ticino*, 6.–15. Juni 2007, S. 70.
2008	Nouveau siège de la Fondation AFLS. In: *AS Architettura Svizzera* 170 (2008), S. 39–40.
	Architetti Tibiletti Associati, Sopraelevazione in via Buffi, Lugano. In: *Archi* 4 (2008), S. 38–41.
	Stefano Tibiletti. Realizzazione progetti in corso 1996–2006. (Vortrag) SUPSI (Scuola universitaria professionale della Svizzera Italiana/Fachhochschule), Manno, Tessin, Januar 2008.
	Dirk Meyhöfer, Casa Duplo. In: Dirk Meyhöfer, *Touch Wood. The Rediscovery of a Building Material*, Salenstein 2008, S. 126–129.
2009	Stefano Tibiletti und Enrico Sassi, Geometrica leggerezza alpina. In: *Casabella* 784 (2009), S. 20–22.
	Houses We Love. Casa Duplo. In: *Dwell+ Magazine* 9/2 (2009), S. 66.
2010	Villa 101, Aldesago. In: *15n sia, la settimana dell'architettura contemporanea*, April/Mai (2010), S. 179.
	Architetti Tibiletti Associati, Casa doppia a Lugano. In: *Archi* 5 (2010), S. 27–31.
	Jacques Gubler, Descente en Lilliput. Fondation alpine pour les Sciences de la vie à Olivone (TI). Tibiletti associati et Enrico Sassi, architectes. In: *FACES* 67 (2010), S. 43–47.
2011	Immeuble d'habitation Beltramina 19a+b. In: *AS Architettura Svizzera* 181 (2011), S. 33–35.
	Residenza per anziani «Gemmo», Edificio d'abitazione «Beltramina». In: *sia, la settimana dell'architettura contemporanea*, April/Mai (2011), TI 14 + TI 15.
	Architetti Tibiletti Associati, Sopraelevare a Lugano. In: *Archi* 6 (2011), S. 56–59.
2012	Villa familiale. In: *AS Architettura Svizzera* 184 (2012), S. 29–30.
	Edificio residenziale a Lugano, Villa unifamiliare a Lugano Aldesago. In: *Katalog Premio SIA Ticino*, 28. Januar–12. Februar 2012, S. 65.
	Via Buffi a Lugano. In: *AS Architettura Svizzera* 186 (2012), S. 35–36.
	Attico Orlandi. In: *sia, la settimana dell'architettura e dell'ingegneria contemporanea*, Mai (2012), TI 06.
	Sede e laboratori AFLS. (Vortrag) zusammen mit Ingenieur Bernasconi, SUPSI (Scuola universitaria professionale della Svizzera Italiana, Fachhochschule), Manno, Tessin, Dezember 2012.
2013	Tibiletti Associati, Abitazioni a Lugano. In: *Archi* 6 (2013), S. 90–95.
	Beltramina Apartment House, Lugano. In: Irma Arribas, Nicola Regusci, Xavier Bustos (Hg.), *Import Ticino: architecture and territory*, Ausst.-Kat. Barcelona 23. Mai–6. Juni 2013, Barcelona 2013, S. 64–67.
	Domenico Lungo, Metamorfosi urbane. Un percorso tra i progetti dello studio Tibiletti Associati. In: *MADE*, 1. Jahrgang, Nr. 0, Juni/Juli 2013, S. 22–26.
2014	Palle Petersen, Naturewuchs un geometrie. In: *Hochparterre*, Dezember 2014, S. 66.
	Arch. Tibiletti Associati Lugano. In: *Ticino Management* 26/4 (2014), S. 52.
	Westside 9. Ristrutturazione stabile e appartamento attico. In: *sia, la settimana dell'architettura e dell'ingegneria contemporanee*, Mai (2014), TI 02 + TI 03.
2015	Mercedes Daguerre, Graziella Zannone Milan, Andrea Pedrazzini (Hg.), *Ticino Guide: architettura e ingegneria*, Zürich 2015.
	Stefano Tibiletti, La costruzione in legno moderna: soluzione interessante per un'architettura di qualità e strutture portanti esigenti. (Vortrag) Accademia di Architettura Mendrisio, Mai 2015.
2016	Ristrutturazione e ampliamento residenza per anziani Gemmo a Lugano, Edificio residenziale Galleria a Lugano. In: *Katalog Premio SIA Ticino 2016*, 27. Februar–6. März 2016, S. 62.
	Ex Municipio Pregassona. In: *Giornate SIA dell'architettura e dell'ingegneria contemporanee*, Mai 2016, S. 220 TI 10.
	Stefano Tibiletti und Catherine Gläser Tibiletti, La trasformazione dell'ex municipio di Pregassona. In: *Archi* 3 (2016), S. 34–37.
	Stefano Tibiletti, Una casa per la terza età. (Vortrag) Istituto internazionale di architettura 12°, Lugano, Juni 2016.
2017	Parkhaus des italienischen Spitals in Lugano. In: *AS Architettura Svizzera* 207 (2017), S. 11–12.
	Stefano Tibiletti, Autosilo Ospedale Italiano di Lugano. In: *Archi* 5 (2017), S. 66–69.
2018	Faire plus grand. Themenheft. *FACES* 74 (2018), S. 42.
2019	Jenny Assi, L'abitare per la terza e la quarta età: from cure to care. In: *Archi* 4 (2019), S. 13–18.
	Catherine Gläser Tibiletti, Abitare bene a tutte le età. Progetto del Quartiere intergenerazionale di Coldrerio. (Vortrag) ATTE (Associazione Ticinese Terza Età), Locarno.

ALBERTO CARUSO (TEXTBEITRAG)

(1945), Architekt, Absolvent des Politecnico di Milano (Technische Hochschule von Mailand), hat in Mailand studiert, führt ein Architekturbüro mit Elisabetta Mainardi. Er hat Projekte in den Zeitschriften *Casabella*, *Domus* und *Zodiac* veröffentlicht. Er ist Mitglied des Bundes Schweizer Architekten (BSA).
996 und 1997 leitete er die Zeitschrift *Rivista Tecnica*, 1998 gründete er *Archi*, die Zeitschrift des schweizerischen Ingenieur- und Architektenvereins, die er bis im Dezember 2017 leitete. 2008 publizierte er das Buch *La resistenza critica del moderno*, Tarmac Publishing Mendrisio.

CLAUDIO FERRATA (TEXTBEITRAG)

Claudio Ferrata ist Geograf, wurde an der Universität Genf zum Doktor der Wirtschafts- und Sozialwissenschaften promoviert und ist im Bereich «Kultur des Territoriums» tätig. Er hat an der Kantonsschule Liceo di Lugano 2 und an der Architekturfakultät des Polytechnikums in Turin unterrichtet. Er ist Autor zahlreicher Studien zu Territoriums- und Landschaftsfragen, seine letzte Arbeit unter dem Titel *Nelle pieghe del Mondo. Il paesaggio negli anni della Convezione europea* ist jüngst bei Meltemi erschienen (2020).

2005	Tibiletti Associati, "Lofts a Lugano". In: *Archi*, July/August, Issue no. 4, p. 40–41
	S. Tibiletti, "La stazione di Lugano". In: *Archi*, May/June, Issue no. 3, p. 28–34
	Conference: "Giornata svizzera dell'energia. Casa Duplo". Conference at the Mendrisio Academy of Architecture
2006	"Mehrfamilienhaus Casa Duplo". In: *AS Architettura Svizzera* 160, p. 39–40
2007	Tibiletti Associati, Casa a Cureglia. In: *Archi* 1, p. 34–37
	"Casa a Cureglia del 2002–2004". In: *Katalog Premio SIA Ticino*, June 6-15 2007, p. 70
2008	Architetti Tibiletti Associati, "Sopraelevazione in via Buffi, Lugano". In: *Archi*, July/August, Issue no. 4, p. 38–41
	S. Tibiletti, "Realizzazione progetti in corso 1996–2006". Conference at SUPSI, January
	D. Meyhöfer, "Simple beauty". In: *touch WOOD – The Rediscovery of a Building Material*, BRAUN, 1st edition
	"Nouveau siège de la Fondation AFLS". In: *AS Architettura Svizzera*, November, Issue no. 170, p. 39–40
2009	S. Tibiletti and E. Sassi, "Geometrica leggerezza alpina". In: *Casabella*, December, Issue no. 784, p. 20–22
	"Houses We Love 'Casa Duplo'". In: *Dwell + Magazine*, December/January, Vol. 9, Issue no. 2, p. 66
2010	Architetti Tibiletti Associati, "Casa doppia a Lugano". In: *Archi*, September/October, Issue no. 5, p. 27–31
	J. Gubler, "Descente en Lilliput, Fondation alpine pour les Sciences de la vie à Olivone (TI). Tibiletti associati et Enrico Sassi, architectes". In: *Faces*, Issue no. 67, p. 43–47
	"Villa 101, Aldesago". In: *sia, la settimana dell'architettura contemporanea*, 15n, April/May, p. 179 TI
2011	Architetti Tibiletti Associati, "Sopraelevare a Lugano". In: *Archi*, December, Issue no. 6, p. 56–59
	"Immeuble d'habitation Beltramina 19a + b". In: *AS Architettura Svizzera*, February, Issue no. 181, p. 33–35
	"Residenza per anziani Gemmo, Edificio d'abitazione Beltramina". In: *sia, La settimana dell'architettura contemporanea*, 2011 edition, April/May, TI 14 + TI 15
2012	Tibiletti and Engineer Bernasconi, "Sede e laboratori AFLS". Conference at SUPSI, December
	"Via Buffi in Lugano". In: *AS Architettura Svizzera*, March, Issue no. 186, p. 35–36
	"Villa familiale". In: *AS Architettura Svizzera*, January, Issue no. 184, p. 29–30
	"Edificio residenziale a Lugano, Villa unifamiliare a Lugano Aldesago". In: *2012 SIA Ticino Award Catalogue*, January 28–February 12, p. 65
	"Attico Orlandi". In: *sia, La settimana dell'architettura e dell'ingegneria contemporanee*, 2012 edition, May, TI 06
2013	Tibiletti Associati, "Abitazioni a Lugano". In: *Archi*, December, Issue no. 6, p. 90–95
	"Beltramina Apartment House, Lugano". In: Irma Arribas, Nicola Regusci, Xavier Bustos (Eds.), *Import Ticino: architecture and territory*, exhib. cat., Barcelona, May 23 – June 6, 2013, Barcelona 2013
	D. Lungo, "Metamorfosi urbane. Un percorso tra i progetti dello studio Tibiletti Associati". In: *MADE*, June/July, Issue no. 0, p. 22–26
2014	P. Petersen, "Naturewuchs und geometrie". In: *Hochparterre*, December, p. 66
	"Arch. Tibiletti Associati Lugano". In: *Ticino Management Year XXVI*, April, Issue no. 4, p. 52
	"Westside9, Ristrutturazione stabile e appartamento attico". In: *sia, La settimana dell'architettura e dell'ingegneria contemporanee*, 2014 edition, May, TI 02 + TI 03
2015	Mercedes Daguerre, G. Zannone Milan, A. Pedrazzini (Eds.), *Ticino Guide: architettura e ingegneria*, Zurich 2015
	S. Tibiletti, "La costruzione in legno moderna: soluzione interessante per un'architettura di qualità e strutture portanti esigenti". Conference at the Mendrisio Academy of Architecture, May
2016	"Ristrutturazione e ampliamento residenza per anziani Gemmo a Lugano, Edificio residenziale Galleria a Lugano". In: *Katalog Premio SIA Ticino 2016*, Febraury 27 – March 6, 2016, p. 62
	"Ex Municipio Pregassona". In: *Giornate SIA dell'architettura e dell'ingegneria contemporanee*, May 2016, p. 220 TI 10
	Stefano Tibiletti and Catherine Gläser Tibiletti, "La trasformazione dell'ex municipio di Pregassona". In: *Archi* 3 (2016), p. 34–37
	Stefano Tibiletti, "Una casa per la terza età". (conference lecture) Istituto internazionale di architettura 12°, Lugano, June 2016
2017	S. Tibiletti, "Autosilo Ospedale Italiano di Lugano". In: *Archi* 5, p. 66–69
	"Parkhaus des italienischen Spitals in Lugano". In: *AS Architettura Svizzera*, April, Issue no. 207, p. 11–12
2018	Cahier Thèmatique, "Faire plus grand". In: *FACES*, autumn, Issue no. 74, p. 42
	C. Ferrata and S. Tibiletti, "Un progetto territoriale per la città di Mendrisio". In: *Archi*, December, Issue no. 6, p. 25–28
2019	J. Assi, "L'abitare per la terza e la quarta età: from cure to care". In: *Archi*, October, Issue no. 4, p. 13–18
	C. Gläser Tibiletti, "Abitare bene a tutte le età, Progetto del Quartiere Intergenrazionale di Coldrerio". Conference for the ATTE Association (Ticinese Third Age Association), Locarno

ALBERTO CARUSO (ARTICLE)

Alberto Caruso (1945), architect, graduated at the Politecnico di Milano, manages an architectural office with Elisabetta Mainardi. He has published projects in the journals *Casabella*, *Domus* and *Zodiac*. He is a member of the Federation of Swiss Architects (BSA).

In 1996 and 1997, he directed the journal *Rivista Tecnica*. In 1998, he founded *Archi*, the journal of the Swiss Association of Engineers and Architects, directing the journal until 2017. In 2008, he published *La resistenza critica del moderno*, Tarmac Publishing Mendrisio.

CLAUDIO FERRATA (ARTICLE)

Claudio Ferrata is a geographer and Professor of Economic and Social Sciences at the University of Geneva. He also works in the field of Territorial Culture. He taught at the Liceo di Lugano 2 and the Faculty of Architecture at the Polytechnic in Turin. He is the author of numerous studies on territorial and landscape issues and his latest essay entitled "Nelle pieghe del Mondo. Il paesaggio negli anni della Convezione europea" was recently published by Meltemi (2020).

FINANZIELLE UND IDEELLE UNTERSTÜTZUNG

Ein besonderer Dank gilt den Institutionen und Sponsorfirmen, deren finanzielle Unterstützungen wesentlich zum Entstehen dieser Buchreihe beitragen. Ihr kulturelles Engagement ermöglicht ein fruchtbares und freundschaftliches Zusammenwirken von Baukultur und Bauwirtschaft.

FINANCIAL AND CONCEPTUAL SUPPORT

Special thanks to our sponsors and institutions whose financial support has helped us so much with the production of this series of books. Their cultural commitment is a valuable contribution to fruitful and cordial collaboration between the culture and economics of architecture.

prohelvetia

Schweizerische Eidgenossenschaft
Confédération suisse
Confederazione Svizzera
Confederaziun svizra

Eidgenössisches Departement des Innern EDI
Bundesamt für Kultur BAK

AB Modelli architettonici, Tesserete

Al Corredo Stefano Colombo & Co. SA, Lugano

Ascensori Falconi SA, Chiasso

Antonio Corti SA, Caslano

Bondini e Colombo Sagl, Lugano

Elettricità Mantegani SA, Lugano

Elettroconsulenze Solcà SA, Lugano

FUTUREDIL Sagl, Balerna

Futurfida SA, Chiasso

GALVOLUX SA, Bioggio

Giugni SA Metalcostruzioni, Locarno

Impresa Barella SA, Chiasso

lacasa interior design sa, Mendrisio

A. Lepori SA Impresa Costruzioni, Lugano

Medici Dario ed Eros, Impresa di costruzioni SA, Morbio Inferiore

Pasi SA, Chiasso

Silvano Pozzi SA, Balerna

Tresoldi Lattonieri SA, Davesco-Lugano

VISANI RUSCONI TALLERI SA, Taverne/Losone

Architetti Tibiletti Associati
88. Band der Reihe De aedibus
Herausgeber: Heinz Wirz, Luzern
Konzept: Heinz Wirz; Architetti Tibiletti Associati, Lugano
Projektleitung: Quart Verlag, Antonia Chavez-Wirz
Textbeiträge: Alberto Caruso, Milano, IT; Claudio Ferrata, Lugano
Objekttexte: Architetti Tibiletti Associati
Textlektorat Deutsch: Kirsten Rachowiak, München, DE
Textlektorat Englisch: Benjamin Liebelt, Berlin, DE
Übersetzung Italienisch–Deutsch: Dr. Eva Dewes, Saarbrücken, DE
Übersetzung Italienisch–Englisch: NTL, Florenz, IT
Fotos: Marcelo Villada Ortiz, Bellinzona; ausser: Filippo Bolognese Images, Milano/Mendrisio S. 56, 57, 68, 69, 71; Alessandro Crinari, Bellinzona S. 26, 27, 29; Swisssurf Sagl, Lugnao S. 33, 34, 35, 39, 40, 43
Redesign: BKVK, Basel – Beat Keusch, Angelina Köpplin-Stützle
Grafische Umsetzung: Quart Verlag
Lithos: Printeria, Luzern
Druck: DZA Druckerei zu Altenburg GmbH, Altenburg, DE

© Copyright 2020
Quart Verlag Luzern, Heinz Wirz
Alle Rechte vorbehalten
ISBN 978-3-03761-203-3

Architetti Tibiletti Associati
Volume 88 of the series De aedibus
Edited by: Heinz Wirz, Lucerne
Concept: Heinz Wirz; Architetti Tibiletti Associati, Lugano
Project management: Quart Verlag, Antonia Chavez-Wirz
Articles by: Alberto Caruso, Milano, IT; Claudio Ferrata, Lugano
Project descriptions: Architetti Tibiletti Associati
German text editing: Kirsten Rachowiak, Munich, DE
English text editing: Benjamin Liebelt, Berlin, DE
Italian–German translation: Dr. Eva Dewes, Saarbrücken, DE
Italian–English translation: NTL, Florence, IT
Photos: Marcelo Villada Ortiz, Bellinzona; except for: Filippo Bolognese Images, Milano/Mendrisio p. 56, 57, 68, 69, 71; Alessandro Crinari, Bellinzona p. 26, 27, 29; Swisssurf Sagl, Lugano p. 33, 34, 35, 39, 40, 43
Redesign: BKVK, Basel – Beat Keusch, Angelina Köpplin-Stützle
Graphic design: Quart Verlag
Lithos: Printeria, Lucerne
Printing: DZA Druckerei zu Altenburg GmbH, Altenburg, DE

© Copyright 2020
Quart Verlag Luzern, Heinz Wirz
All rights reserved
ISBN 978-3-03761-203-3

Quart Verlag GmbH
Denkmalstrasse 2, CH-6006 Luzern
books@quart.ch, www.quart.ch

De aedibus
Des architectes contemporains et leurs travaux

De aedibus
Contemporary architects and their buildings

88	Architetti Tibiletti Associati (de/en)	44	Luca Deon (de/en)
87	Zach + Zünd (de/en)	43	2b (de/en)
86	Kistler Vogt (de/en)	42	Durisch + Nolli (de/en)
85	Sylla Widmann (de/en, fr/en)	41	sabarchitekten (de/en)
84	Aebi & Vincent Architekten (de/en)	40	Beat Rothen (de/en)
83	Baumberger & Stegmeier (de/en)	39	Atelier Bonnet (de/en)
82	L-architectes (de/en, de/fr)	38	Novaron (de/en)
81	Frei Rezakhanlou (de/en)	37	Althammer Hochuli (de/en)
80	weberbrunner (de/en)	36	Schneider & Schneider (de/en)
79	Meyer Piattini (de/en)	35	Frei & Ehrensperger (de und en)
78	meier + associés architectes (de/en, de/fr)	34	Liechti Graf Zumsteg (de/en)
77	Lin Robbe Seiler (de/en, de/fr)	33	Adrian Streich (de/en)
76	Meier Leder (de/en)	32	Daniele Marques (de/en)
75	Butikofer de Oliveira Vernay (de/en)	31	Neff Neumann (de/en)
74	Elisabeth & Martin Boesch (de/en)	30	Giraudi Wettstein (de/en)
73	spaceshop Architekten (de/en)	29	Steinmann & Schmid (de/en)
72	Kast Kaeppeli (de/en)	28	Matthias Ackermann (de/en)
71	Philippe Meyer (de/en, fr)	27	Aeby & Perneger (de/en)
70	bartbuchhofer (de/en)	26	Bakker & Blanc (de/en)
69	Hauenstein La Roche Schedler (de/en)	25	Markus Wespi Jérôme de Meuron (de/en)
68	Graeme Mann & Patricia Capua Mann (de/en)	24	Bauart (de/en, de/fr)
67	Esposito Javet (de/en, de/fr)	23	Knapkiewicz & Fickert (de/en)
66	Galletti Matter (de/en, de/fr)	22	Marcel Ferrier (de/en)
65	Fruehauf, Henry & Viladoms (de/en)	21	Wild Bär Architekten (de/en)
64	Jakob Steib (de/en)	20	Enzmann + Fischer (de/en)
63	bunq (de/en)	19	Mierta und Kurt Lazzarini (de/en)
62	Jean-Paul Jaccaud (de/en, de/fr)	18	Rolf Mühlethaler (de/en)
61	huggenbergerfries (de/en)	17	Pablo Horváth (de/en)
60	Berrel Berrel Kräutler (de/en)	16	Brauen + Wälchli (de/en)
59	Pierre-Alain Dupraz (de/en, de/fr)	15	E2A Eckert Eckert Architekten (de/en)
58	Cometti Truffer (de/en)	14	Lussi + Halter (de/en)
57	Joos & Mathys (de/en)	13	Philipp Brühwiler (de/en)
56	Lacroix Chessex (de/en)	12	Scheitlin – Syfrig + Partner (de/en)
55	Savioz Fabrizzi (de/en)	11	Vittorio Magnago Lampugnani (de/en)
54	Boegli Kramp (de/en)	10	Bonnard Woeffray (de/en und de/fr)
53	Zita Cotti (de/en)	9	Graber Pulver (de/en)
52	Oestreich + Schmid (de/en)	8	Burkhalter Sumi / Makiol Wiederkehr (de/en)
51	Stump & Schibli Architekten (de/en)	7	Gigon/Guyer (de und en)
50	Luca Gazzaniga (de/en)	6	Andrea Bassi (de, fr und en)
49	Guignard & Saner (de/en)	5	Dieter Jüngling und Andreas Hagmann (de und en)
48	Morger + Dettli (de/en)	4	Beat Consoni (de und en)
47	Charles Pictet (de/en)	3	Max Bosshard & Christoph Luchsinger (de)
46	Armando Ruinelli + Partner (de/en/it)	2	Miroslav Šik (de, en und it)
45	Luca Selva Architekten (de/en)	1	Valentin Bearth & Andrea Deplazes (de, en und it)

books@quart.ch, www.quart.ch